LOVE'S MIRROR

An Anthology of Short Stories

By

MICHAEL PATRICK MURRAY

******

This book is a work of fiction. Places, events, and situations in this story are purely fictional. Any resemblance to actual persons, living or dead, is coincidental.

ISBN: 1-4033-7128-8 (e-book)
ISBN: 1-4033-7129-6 (Paperback)
ISBN: 1-4033-7130-X (Dust Jacket)

This book is printed on acid free paper.

1stBooks - rev. 03/17/03

She whom I love is neither saint nor sinner

But a wild creature unashamed of truth

Edward Bulwer-Lytton

******

For those whose love is reflected here

Stories

HONEY AND THE SOLDIER

It was a comfortable Saturday night in Kansas that June 24th in 1950. But comfortable or not, the soldier who walked toward a run down bar and dance hall believed that this particular evening in Junction City, not far from Fort Riley, was probably the worst place to be. Except, that is, for any other night in Junction City in 1950. At that moment it was already Sunday, June 25th in Korea, some 13 hours ahead of eastern daylight saving time in Washington, D.C. A fateful time for the soldier. He just didn't know it then.

Fort Riley, where the soldier was assigned, was the post where the late George Armstrong Custer's horse had lived out its life; the only survivor of Custer's egregious last stand. This Custer was not the General Custer, as myth would have us believe. But rather the arrogant, Lieutenant Colonel George Armstrong Custer, who died foolishly seeking glory at Little Big Horn. His horse lived well at Fort Riley for many years after that infamous battle.

As legendary as Fort Riley was, that lovely old Army fort left much to be desired. Starting with women. Of which there were far too few. And which dearth of this most important specie was exacerbated by the presence of many dogface soldiers. Of which there were too damn many.

Under the circumstances who would expect a 19 year old basic trainee from the 10th Infantry Division - the fine old 10th Mountain Division - to be thrown together with a lovely lady, also nineteen years young, in a seedy dance hall crowded with about 500 soldiers and maybe a dozen girls, if that many.

The green soldier, then in his twelfth week of basic, had no expectations except to con a few beers out of consistently lax bartenders whose motto was, "If they are in uniform and have a pulse, never check I.D."

The soldier's intended beer consumption was coupled with the idea that it might at least be fun to watch some of the young women who hung around the dump from time to time being rushed to exhaustion by a queue of soldiers who cut in not much after the guy ahead of them got a couple of moments of dancing before having to surrender his prize. But watching got old quickly for the soldier, and he soon discovered that watching wasn't really his game. And the urge to hold a young, soft girl in his arms compelled him to join the procession of hopeful Army neophytes. He grudgingly got in line and finally was able to cut in and embrace the loveliest woman in the world. Well, at least the loveliest in Junction City, at that moment. "I've been in this Army town a dozen times, and it's always the same. Too many guys, not enough girls, but my luck just might change," he said to himself.

Never one to stand on ceremony, the soldier, after a few dance steps while delighting in the feel of the lovely lady's warm, and oh so lush and nicely proportioned body, looked her squarely in the eyes and said, "This is nuts, unless you like being mauled by horny dog soldiers. So why don't you and I get out of here, and go somewhere quiet where we can talk and get to know each other without a zillion other guys grabbing at you, with all kinds of bad intentions. I have no phony designs. So we'll go someplace where you can feel safe and you can tell me to bug off anytime you suspect I am getting out of line. I'm really serious about this. I don't know anyone in this lonely town except the guys I am training with. I'm not going to let a chance to know someone I sense is very special like you, just to con you into letting me jump your bones and mess everything up just when we were getting to know each other."

"Oh, God, that sounds good," the lady immediately and gratefully replied. "I had no idea it was going to be a madhouse when my friend and I stopped in to do some dancing. I'll tell her I'm leaving and see what she wants to do. Come along, or what. O.K?"

The soldier said great, and with that the lady broke away and went over to her friend who was looking apprehensively at the line of soldiers approaching her and her dance partner of the moment. She readily accepted the idea that leaving was the best thing she could do since no one she might have been interested in had approached her with any proposition except, "Let's get it on somewhere, like in the back seat of my Chevy."

The two girls and the soldier then left, much to the dismay of several hundred guys in brown uniforms, which uniforms sadly reflected young, and only slightly trained soldiers. So many, so far from home, and lonely as hell, who had no way of knowing that they would soon find themselves in an even more distant place called Korea, where a war had just begun that very day as the North Korean Peoples Army (NKPA) invaded South Korea. Young men, whose training in the 10th Infantry Division for a possible war, would become reality in a few weeks far from the safe hills of Fort Riley and the great State of Kansas.

Fortunately the other girl had a car since the soldier had none, and they drove across town to an all night coffee shop near the hotel where the girls were staying in a nicer part of Junction City, if there was such a part in 1950. They got something to eat and talked for a long time. Until, that is, the inevitable moment arrived when three single souls evolved into a crowd, and the other girl generously suggested that she should be getting along since she wanted to be in church in the morning for the nine a.m. Methodist service.

The soldier promised to take his date home in a cab, and assured the other girl that his date would be all right and would return both safe and sound. He wasn't thinking in terms of anything more than a little more precious time with the lovely, young woman, whose name he decided was going to be Honey no matter what her folks had Christened her some 19 years earlier. She didn't seem to mind. So they left it at that, although she insisted on calling the soldier by his given name, Michael.

They stayed a while in the coffee shop, making small talk and drinking a bit too much coffee, which got them both a bit wired on caffeine. Honey related how she was born and raised in a small town. Small was a euphemism for a tiny hamlet that had not even one stoplight. After graduating from the county public high school, she worked for a while in a local general store to save money for college. But, as is natural under such restricting conditions, she grew bored and decided to hook up with a group of young people who had been recruited to be part of a traveling magazine sales troop out of Tennessee, whose strange itinerary would take them through the Midwest and maybe all the way to the West coast.

This is what brought Honey to Junction City and a fateful meeting with a soldier named Michael in June 1950. Michael told her he was born and raised in Wisconsin, and joined the Army after two years of college because he was broke and realized he was too young when he started at the university at age 17. He joined to take advantage of the G.I Bill, which he would use to finish college, and maybe to grow up a bit at the same time. Not so jokingly, he admitted that he was 17 going on 12, when he started on the path of higher learning. "I found myself at a major university, with several thousand other students. But the real shocker was that I discovered I was surrounded by a host of returning World War II vets, male and female, who had seen more of life in four years of war than I had experienced in seventeen years on the planet," Michael said rather wistfully. "Thus after two years of competing with men and women who were far ahead in the game of life, I decided to add some more maturity to my own existence, and opted for the regimen of being a soldier for a while. Didn't know if it was a good idea until now and I got the chance to meet you, and now I think it was a great idea, and I'm sure glad I decided to come into town tonight.

"I'm awfully glad you did, Michael," Honey interjected, displaying a genuine and disarming smile. "Otherwise I wouldn't have met you, and Junction City would be just another stopover in Kansas in my search to discover what else life can offer outside of Nowhere, Tennessee, which is what I call my hometown which is, in truth, just a village."

"Well, Honey, that makes two of us who are happy I joined the U.S. Army, although there have been times in these past few months that I thought maybe I should have become a Marine since this man's army has way too damn many draftees, most of whom would rather be anywhere else, instead of suffering basic training army style. But most important is that whatever crap I've had to put up with in the

Army, I got to meet you, and that wonderful coincidence makes every other bad minute worth it and then some."

"Such a smooth talker you are," Honey said smiling. "I do believe you mean what you are saying, even if I am little naïve at times. Small town girl and all. But I accept your gracious compliment, although I'm not sure how I can repay such nice flattery, which I do accept as sincere." Honey looked at Michael with clearly no pretense in her genuine interest in him.

"Hey, it's sincere. No bull. You are the nicest thing that ever happened to me. Truly. And in answer to your problem, I can think of a couple things you could do to repay the compliment," Michael replied with a grin that barely concealed his hopes of being able to spend some time playing kissy face and engaging in a whole lot of delightful petting with the lady. "But I said I'd stay on my best behavior, and I want to see you again, so I'm sure as hell not going to screw up now and scare you off first thing out of the box."

"I'm not afraid, Michael," Honey responded softly, looking at her young man without any sense of disbelief. "I didn't think you would hustle me and I sensed you were different than the ton of guys who were bent on attacking me every which way at that sad awful dance hall. Which makes it a little strange now because I'm not entirely certain I would want to resist your advances. And this is not like me at all." Michael looked into Honey's lovely green eyes and chose not to reply for a moment because he wanted to come across sincerely."Wow," Michael then said as genuinely as possible, "I don't want to presume Honey anything you might object to, but I'm flattered that you aren't afraid of me and that the future might hold a promise of a more intimate relationship you wouldn't resist."

"O.K, enough of this sparring around," Honey said while flashing that same lovely smile Michael had been relishing all evening. "Let me ask you something, and it is not intended to embarrass but rather only to lay the groundwork so to speak. And no pun is intended."

"Hey, no problem. Ask away."

"O.K.," Honey began. "Straight out. Are you a virgin?"

"Yep," Michael replied. "I suppose I should fake it and pretend to be a man with a lot of sexual experience. But it would be bullshit. I have never had sexual intercourse with a woman or anything else, which sounds a little weird now that I say it. But I haven't. And virgin is an understatement in my case." Michael admitted this, a little embarrassed, but wanting to be truthful at the same time.

"Well, so far so good," Honey said smiling again, "because I too am a virgin. I know that sounds strange, but I really was a country bumpkin, and while I had a lot of pressure exerted over the past few years to give up my virginity, and no bad jokes, please, about Tennessee hillbillies all being related, I have held out. Not necessarily for marriage, but just because I wanted to feel good about the guy I surrendered to, and, frankly, I hadn't met him as yet. But the reason for asking if you are a virgin is that I think … maybe … and this is really out of character for me, I think that I have finally met someone who I can relate to in an instinctive way, even though I've only known you for a few hours, and, in so many ways, I don't know much about you at all. But I get a sense that maybe, just maybe, this would be as good a time as any to find out if I wanted to be less a virgin in the morning and would not regret it if we spent the night together."

"Gosh, Honey," Michael exclaimed, more than a little surprised, and not certain if he had gotten Honey's meaning right. "I really don't know how to react, and I sure as hell don't want to mess up this moment. I can only say that if you are willing to spend the night with me, and I hope this means making love with you, then I can assure you that nothing, and I do mean - nothing – would make me happier.

The Irish leprechauns - the ones who watch over love and war - are surely on my side tonight. Not that I'm superstitious, mind you, but I'm not going to tempt fate. And if the little people are content by having brought us together, far be it from me to doubt their kindness and wisdom. I am just so delighted to have met you, and for the chance to know you intimately and lovingly.

"But only one thing … and I'm a little embarrassed to admit this but I've got to be honest, I don't know a damn thing about lovemaking. Oh sure, I've done my share of necking and playing touchy feely with girls here and there. Copping a feel or two and then maybe some manual exploring to go along with it, but I've never had intercourse, and I'm afraid I might not be any good at it. I would really hate to disappoint you. This is very important to me for both our sakes."

"Certainly that's a consideration, Michael, but I'm willing to find out," Honey answered with sincerity. "And I doubt if I will be disappointed if we work on this together. I have a book. It came from Europe. I got it from a girl in the group who she said she got it underground because it can't be sold here in the USA. It explains all kinds of things that they never taught us in school, and suggests techniques that a man and woman can experiment with so that each is satisfied with their mutual lovemaking.

“I think you are sensitive and will not only be gentle with me, but will be open to experiment and suggestion. So I'm not afraid of your inexperience, or of mine. In fact, I think it's an advantage, because we can make love in a considerate way because we want to be together as fully as possible and we are willing not to rush it. I'm certain this will not be just a one night stand where the guy is into nothing more than wham bam, and, if you are lucky, he'll add 'thank you, ma'am,' but nothing more would ever be offered."

"Yeah, I know. Not that I've been one of those jerks, but I know the type. I see 'em everyday, or hear 'em talking about the scores they made over a weekend. But none of them can remember even one name of the generous girls they used. I promise you I will say thank you, and better still, I will remain eternally grateful. I think I'm damn lucky to be with you, and to share this new experience."

"O.K soldier, I believe you. So let's get marching before I lose my nerve. And by the way where are we going to go?" Honey asked realizing for the first time they couldn't go to the hotel where the group was staying, and they didn't know about any other place they might otherwise go.

"I don't know, but I've got a month's pay with me. A whole $75.00. Can you believe how well they pay buck privates?" Michael answered sarcastically. "So I'll slip outside and ask a taxi driver where a reasonably nice place would be for us to spend the night. You wait right here. Be right back," he added as he headed for the door and a taxi stand near the coffee shop. He returned in a minute and said, "I've got a cab out front. The driver said he could take us to a nice place, but it's in a somewhat darker part of town. He said that wouldn't be a problem, however, and there was nothing to worry about. Besides he says the price would be right. O.K.?"

"Sure, why not, as long as it's nice. Doesn't matter if it's on the other side of the tracks. Right?" Honey replied with a smile.

The cabbie took them first to the hotel where Honey's group was staying, and she went inside to get the European sex book about how to do all sorts of wonderful things between a man and a woman, as well as to advise her roommate she would not be back tonight. When she did, there were no questions asked, and there were no looks of disapproval. Her roommate just silently understood and said something to the effect that Honey was a lucky girl because Michael seemed nice, and hoped she would have lots of fun.

When Honey returned to the cab, Michael told her the cabbie said the cost of the room would be four dollars, and he had to get the key from the guy who lives in a house nearby and manages the motel type place where they were going to spend the night. It was like the cabins one sees along Route 66, and many other highways. The deal was made and the cabbie gave Michael the key after arriving at a clean looking set of single, albeit very small, one story structures.

The cab fare was one dollar. Michael tipped the guy an extra dollar for being so nice.

Then he and Honey went inside their "bridal suite" on the outskirts of the colored area of Junction City. Michael said, "Maybe I should carry you across the threshold," but Honey suggested that he should save his energy with a promise that he was going to need it.

They explored their new digs and found it to contain a bedroom that doubled as a living room, along with a bathroom, and a little kitchen/dinette area not much bigger than a closet. But, all and all, it was cozy and inviting. Michael observed, "Hey all the comforts of home. And a whole lot better than the open barracks I live in with fifty other noisy guys. This is like a Taj Mahal by comparison."

They stood silently for a moment, each feeling a bit awkward. Then Michael chuckled, "By the way, you know I've never even kissed you and here we are about to embark on something substantially more involved than just kissing. Maybe we should kiss for openers and proceed slowly from there."

"Good idea," Honey replied as Michael gathered her in his arms and then kissed her tenderly at first and then passionately as a follow up.

"Wow," Honey sighed. "And you thought I might not like the way you kiss. I don't think we are going to have any trouble with the rest since you are better than good at this kissy face stuff."

"Why, thank you, Ma'am. Lots more where that came from, but I'd better go slow. You know what they say about teenaged males who are hornier than a bag of toads, or want of more picturesque expression, hornier than a three-peckered billy goat. Horny and then some. So if I get too rambunctious, just slow me down.

"How about we finish that dance we started way back in the evening at the dance hall?"

"Good idea, Michael. It is better to go a bit slow, I think, and it will help us get over any shyness that is normal at a time like this," Honey said with a big smile.

With that Michael turned on the radio and tuned to a romantic music station. He took Honey in his arms and they danced, fully clothed, on the linoleum floor, which was better than a rug to dance on, and besides, there weren't any rugs. They glided around the room slowly with occasional pauses for some delicious kisses as a growing passion heightened in both of them. Honey pressed herself against Michael, and she felt his erection that was clearly evident. He held her closer and then, without a word, he loosened her blouse and lifted it over her head and casually tossed it on the bed. Honey did not resist as he then unhooked her bra and allowed her lovely breasts to be exposed. He wanted to devour them, but he restrained himself as he took off his uniform jacket and then his uniform shirt and tie, and tee-shirt, while still keeping up a semblance of the slow dancing.

He felt her skin on his and the passion they each were clearly feeling, so he tried to steel himself against the urge to put Honey on the bed and take her virginity without further preliminaries. Honey sensed his desire, which matched hers. But she accepted that this was their first time, and she thought they should have some idea beyond animal instinct on how to do it right. So she stepped back and suggested that they get naked and sit down on the bed for a moment and look at the sex manual and see if they could figure out the best way to proceed.

Michael needed no further prodding as to the naked part, and they each slipped out of their remaining clothing. Then Michael said, "Let's dance a bit more like this. It's really sexy and I love holding you without any clothes. Don't let my protuberance get in the way. It's just part of the ritual. You know the old joke, the lightest thing in the world is a penis, even a thought can raise it," he added with a big grin.

As they danced naked, Michael was certain - in that most glorious moment - that he loved Honey beyond all reason. But then no nineteen-year-old male has ever been able to reason with an erection. So he simply chose to surrender to a willingness to love her with total abandon. At nineteen he wasn’t certain what all was involved in that, but he knew he felt damn good about it.

Honey stood five foot seven in her bare feet, and fit nicely up against Michael's six feet. He thought she looked a lot like his favorite movie star, Eleanor Parker, but Honey had long brown hair instead of red. A close resemblance was there, however, with her beautiful eyes and perfect nose and chin. And he decided that the lovely green eyed lady, with the incredible smile and wonderful body, was maybe even more beautiful than Eleanor, which he had to admit was going some considering Eleanor Parker's great beauty.

They danced a bit more, and then Michael eased them towards the bed, and propped up some pillows so they could read the forbidden how to book from Europe together, and get a few ideas on how to make love for the first time without screwing up. He thought without verbalizing his concern, as they settled comfortably side-by-side, “The screwing part is apropos, but I sure as hell don’t want to fuck it up. And the pun is intentional.”

The first chapter was dedicated to foreplay, and although experienced with fellatio which a couple of girls had performed on him when he was in high school, Michael had never thought of reciprocating in turn, so the word cunnilingus was new to him, as was the idea.

He asked Honey if that seemed like something she might be interested in, and if they should give it a try. Honey replied, "Well my love, I don't have any more experience with this than you do, but it sure looks interesting and exciting, so why don't we have a go at it, and I take you, and you take me at the same time as the picture suggests, and we can see what it's like."

They did. It was wonderful, of course. So much so that they had to slow down in order to return to the book for further suggestions. Michael was curious about the clitoris as an erogenous zone and precisely how much dedication should be addressed to it, so Honey explained as she guided his hand to the precise spot, "This is where it really counts in spite of claims of vaginal orgasm versus clitoral."

"God, do I love touching you," Michael exclaimed.

"God, do I love you touching me," Honey responded ecstatically.

Then they experimented a little more with substantial success and ultimately each surrendered their virginity to the other. And having disciplined themselves to wait for this ultimate moment through gentle and loving foreplay, they found mutual release and satisfaction as they happily left their innocence behind in a most meaningful way. They lay in each other's arms afterwards, with Honey clinging to Michael as if trying to crawl inside of him, and he delighted in her display of need and the appreciation for the fine man she had waited for the first nineteen years of her life. Then they fell asleep, and awoke after a while, and loved again. After which they slept some more, and awakened to a reprise of their earlier passion and made love once again, and once more after that, for a total of four wonderful sessions of young, energetic coupling and unselfish exchanging of loving responses. "I'm so delighted to have made love with you for my first time," Michael said most sincerely. "Only wish we had more time. I hate to ever let you go"

At twelve noon they got up and showered together holding each other tenderly as the warm water flowed over their nakedness like a blessing on their love. They were supposed to vacate the cabin by one p.m., so when that unwelcome hour arrived, they reluctantly prepared to leave. They looked around the room and at the bed without speaking. But they each shared the same sentiment that, although they had to return to the real world of everyday mundane living, the magic of the cabin would be forever preserved in tender memory and with no regrets whatsoever.

"I know it's a bit soon to being saying something as serious as I love you, but I do. And I don't mean that I just think I do. Because I really do, and I am damn certain I always will. The spiritual people who believe in reincarnation talk about meeting one's soul mate. I thought it was a lot of bunk, but now I know what they mean. You are my soul mate, and I love you, I love you, I love you. So you can take that to the bank. We are joined forever. And that's a promise."

Honey looked at Michael with a wonder and love he could feel deep in his soul. Something he could not explain to anyone who hasn't been there.

"I know, my love. I know," Honey breathed softly. "And if there were words beyond even saying, I love you too, intensely and forever, I would use them. But sometimes it is the simple truth in life that is the strongest and says it best. I love you, and I know now that I have never loved anyone before you. And I never will love anyone else, no matter what. I am so happy we found each other and are able to do this again and again."

The last part, where Honey added no matter what, struck fear in Michael's heart, but he dared not ask what she could possibly mean by that, so he said nothing. Instead he took her in his arms and said, "Let's have one last dance before we have to leave paradise for a while. But I do swear there will be other places for us my dearest love, and we will have a lifetime of love and being one together. We are soul mates. And I mean eternally."

They danced and kissed as they waited for a cab to go back to the coffee shop where they had been the night before to have lunch and just enjoy themselves until Michael had to catch a bus back to Fort Riley to return to his unit, Company B, 85th Infantry, 10th Infantry Division, by midnight.

After a long lunch they spent the rest of the day slowly walking hand in hand and talking and making plans for the future, stopping a whole lot for some hugs and kisses, each with more longing and a tinge of sadness as the time approached for Michael to head back to the Fort. Honey accompanied him to the bus station and would take a cab back to the hotel after his bus pulled out.

Their final, lingering kiss of the day was exchanged as if they were alone in the world and there weren't dozens of other soldiers around wishing to hell they were like Michael and wondering why he didn't just go over the hill and run as far away as possible with the gorgeous creature he was painfully having to say goodbye to. Honey had told him that her group was going to be in Junction City for three more days and then in Manhattan, Kansas, for four days after that. He could call her at the hotel any evening, and she would also leave the number of the hotel where they would be in Manhattan. This way they could make plans for their next loving reunion, hopefully on the coming weekend. Michael vowed that neither proverbial hell nor high water would keep them apart, and he would call and call until he heard her voice again. He emphasized that he loved her so much he could die on the spot for having to leave her for even a minute, much less a week.

"I love you, dear lady," were the last words he was able to say to Honey through the open window of the bus as it took him away from her on its terrible mission to bring him and the other, soon to be trained, warriors closer to the violence that shortly would be visited upon them and thousands of other soldiers, Marines, airmen, and sailors in a far off land. Honey had never even heard of a place called Korea until they had caught a brief news flash over the radio about some people called the NKPA (North Korean People's Army) who had crossed over the 38th parallel into the South Korean peninsula and launched a surprise attack against ROK (Republic of Korea) troops.

*****

On Monday morning, Company B fell out for reveille and roll call. Daylight had come on slowly, but the sun could now be seen creeping above the hills towards the east, and Michael prepared himself for the final week of basic training without giving the Army much other thought, since his concentration was entirely on Honey's face, and body, and smell, and taste. So it came as a surprise when the Company Commander, who seldom took reveille, walked out in front of the company following roll call and announced that certain changes were in progress.

"For openers men, you have arrived at the end of your basic training, even though it is a few days short of a normal session. The reason is that a war has broken out in South Korea between the North and South, and the United States forces stationed there are in need of help and reinforcement as they get a whole lot closer and closer to direct involvement. So we are elected to be part of that help since we are the company most advanced in the basic training cycle."

“What the hell is he talking about?” Michael silently wondered. “For Christ sake why change things now? This is scary shit. Are we moving out? Why now, just when I want to stay close to wherever Honey is going to be. Hell I was going to ask her to leave the group and stay in Manhattan so we could be together every day once basic was finished. Now what the hell is happening? I finally thought this

Army stuff isn't too bad, and then this shit has to happen. This better not interfere with me and Honey, just when we finally found each other. God how I love her. The Army better not fuck up our lives. I'll soldier with the best of them, but no way can I put Honey in second place in my life."

"The company cadre will be directing your movements for the rest of the day," the Company Commander continued. "You will start with returning to your barracks following breakfast. And, after that, you will proceed directly to your squads, and start packing all of your personal gear and uniforms. All company training gear will be returned to company supply before 1000 hours. At which time you will be packed and ready to proceed as directed. Anyone with a personal automobile will take it prior to that time to the Provost Marshall impound lot and it will be left there after signing in until further orders. No vehicles will be left in the company area or on the base except in the impound lot. They will be secure until you return to pick them up at such time as is determined appropriate."

"Damn, this sounds really serious," he said to himself, with more than a little alarm. "I've got to get to a phone somehow. I've got to let Honey know that things are suddenly SNAFU and I'll get in touch with her as soon as I can. From wherever. If I miss her at either of the hotels, I will write to her home address in Tennessee."

Things went from bad to worse from that point, and with the rest of Company B, Michael followed orders, the most serious of which was to fully pack his duffle bag with whatever would fit, and deep six the rest. He didn't have a car to worry about, but it was obvious that he could only pack what military clothing and other necessary gear he could, and along with his Garand rifle, be ready to mount out at 1000 hours. After packing his duffle, he slipped out of the barracks, ostensibly in order to take his "nonexistent" car to the PMO impound lot, and ran as fast as he could to the Service Club to call Honey at her hotel.

She was out selling magazines, but the clerk promised faithfully that he would give her a message, and he did. When Honey returned later that afternoon she got Michael's message about there being a big change in his training and it looked like he was being shipped to another base. He would contact her as soon as he could, and, if he missed her in Junction City and/or Manhattan, he would write to her in Tennessee and would soon let her know where he was. And most of all he loved her very much and this screw up by the Army will soon pass and they will be together again. So she was not to worry. Everything was going to be all right, and he would keep her posted on where he was and what was happening.

That was it. And as he feared, Michael was not able to reach Honey by phone before she finished her sales trip in Manhattan. Her next stop was Wichita, but he didn't know it. His next stop was a replacement depot in California, where he was sent by troop train for further processing and ultimate deployment to South Korea. He had no way of calling for the next week, and by then Honey had moved on with the magazine tour, so he wrote to her at her home in Tennessee. He didn't have a reliable address for her to write back, however, so he said he would write some more when he was with a more permanent unit in Korea, and they could finally make some sense out of all this frustration.

Processing at the replacement depot in California took less than one week. They got a lot of immunization shots to prepare them for whatever diseases they might encounter along the Yellow Sea, which may have been for the better. But seven shots in five days made Michael's arms and buttocks hurt like hell, and rendered them damn near useless for a couple of days. Nevertheless, he and the others survived this initial assault on their well-being, and were flown to South Korea, arriving in country in early July. Which was not a minute too soon because several Army units from the U.S. 24th Division had made contact with the enemy. They were getting their asses kicked in spite of heroics by some veterans of World War II, and some of the mostly green, ill-prepared, peacetime, occupation soldiers as the American forces found themselves fully engaged in the so-called police action, more realistically known as the Korean War. Task Force Smith from the 24th Division was decimated in its early contacts with the enemy in bloody fighting, and the entire division had to ultimately be rescued and given time to catch its breath with the landing of the U.S. 25th Division between July 10th and 15th, and the lst Cavalry on July 18th.

Michael was assigned to the 25th Division, and became a rifleman in Dog Company, lst Battalion. His unit was immediately put on the line, and then thrust into the fray, especially after the 24th Infantry Regiment broke and fled in the face of fierce enemy action on July 20th.

All this time Michael had no opportunity to receive any mail from Honey, but he was able to write some letters and send her a general mailing address just before he left California where she could write to him with at least a Division and Army Post Office (APO, San Francisco) designation, even though he didn't know what battalion or company he would be assigned to until he arrived in Korea. Honey got the address, and sent several letters to Michael over the next weeks, but it took a while for them to catch up with his precise unit, and he never got them before he was seriously wounded and evacuated to Japan for a year's hospitalization.

His almost fatal wounds came about as a result of a terrifying engagement with the enemy on July 30th. The day before he had risked life and limb, above and beyond the call of duty by leaving the marginal safety of a small foxhole and rushing out, without being told to do so, or being told not to do so, to save three of his companions who had been cut off in a forward outpost. Realizing that the men were in imminent danger of death if something wasn't done, Michael ran forward of the defensive line and he headed for an NKPA machine gun emplacement that had pinned down the three soldiers in the outpost and was bent on killing them. He was hit in the left arm before he'd gotten very far, but this didn't stop him. It actually gave him more determination to kick the asses of the gooks, as the enemy were angrily called, who clearly were opposing his mission of mercy.

In spite of his recklessness and wound, Michael managed to get close enough to throw several grenades into the open machine gun bunker. Then he charged and found that he had killed three NKPA soldiers, and the American soldiers were able to withdraw from the outpost and return to lines set up by Michael's company.

His wound was treated, but because it was not considered debilitating, he was allowed to remain on the line. The next day his heroics were repeated during a brutal mortar attack by the NKPA in which a combat patrol was pinned down as they scouted the forward edges of the lines - the so-called no man's land in military jargon that came out of World War I - when the barrage caught them flat footed.

Michael saw two men obviously badly wounded by a mortar shell that hit within 35 yards of their position, and once again he left the safety of his foxhole and ran to the men to help them withdraw to safety. He couldn't handle them both at once, so he picked up the one who seemed to be worse off and literally carried him back to the defensive lines. Then, in spite of strong suggestion by the platoon sergeant that he get his ass down and there would be no more going forward during the barrage, he ran out again to save the second soldier. As he lifted the wounded man, another mortar round came crashing in, and, if it were not for the amount of metal absorbed by the second wounded man he was lifting, Michael would have been torn to bits. He was severely wounded, however, and both he and his comrade went down in a tangle of arms, legs, mangled flesh, and blood. They remained in that horrible condition until the mortar attack lifted and his unit was able to advance beyond the point where Michael and his now dead companion were lying.

The company medic checked both Michael and the other soldier and concluded that they were both dead, so he rolled them together in a poncho and left them for graves registration personnel who would follow up. 13 hours later, Michael and the dead soldier were transported to the Graves Registration Center at battalion. Only then, as the poncho was fully unwrapped, was it discovered that Michael wasn't dead, although he probably would be soon without immediate attention. But he was still alive and a medical evacuation chopper was called in and he was transported to a MASH field surgical unit where he underwent extensive surgery for multiple wounds. Two days later he was further evacuated to a hospital ship, and then later to the U.S.

Naval Hospital in Yokuska, Japan, which was best equipped to provide additional surgery and care for all seriously wounded service personnel of any branch as might be necessary. For reasons which are only known to the gods of confusion who enjoy imposing the ultimate SNAFU on heroes in war, Michael's unit was advised that he had been killed in action. And that is how they ran him on the unit diary and morning report.

They didn't learn for several weeks that actually he was still alive. But before then, fate had taken another terrible turn in the lives of Honey and Michael. Six of Honey's letters finally caught up with Michael's unit, but of course he wasn't there is get them, and he was thought to have been killed in action. His company commander would ordinarily merely have had an army postal unit return them to the sender with the notation deceased on the envelope. But Michael had been twice a hero, and his company commander recommended him, at that time he believed posthumously, for award of the Distinguished Service Cross, the second highest medal for bravery in the Army, and a Silver Star, along with two Purple Hearts, all of which would eventually be awarded to Michael many months later as he slowly recovered from his physical and emotional wounds.

The latter, less readily apparent wounds, were bifurcated between his mistaken belief that Honey didn't love him after all, and the terror of being at all times fully aware that he was alive and was wrapped for 13 hours in a poncho with a very dead companion. Thus, the company commander went one step further than usual and personally returned all of Honey's six, unopened letters to her with a note detailing the heroic conduct of Michael and said that he sincerely regretted having to inform her that Michael had lost his life. But he was proud that it was as a result of his dedicated and totally unselfish sacrifice for others and his country.

Honey was devastated when she received her returned letters and the commanding officer's note of sympathy. And she was most distressed because she realized he never got to read her letters and know how much she missed him, and loved him, and would forever.

She wanted Michael to know that she would wait as long as it took for him to return home to her and their love. Now she sadly and painfully had to accept that now he never would. She kept the letters he had sent her, along with the six she had written that were returned to her, placing them lovingly and carefully in small jewelry chest. She only opened the box when she felt his spiritual presence and needed to reread his words of love over and over.

Adding to the ironical confusion over his presumed death was the failure of anyone from the Army to correct the misinformation about his presumed death, and Honey was never told that Michael was not dead, but rather, was recovering slowly at the Naval Hospital in Japan. He had first come out of a semi-coma, which had lasted several weeks after he had been wounded that fateful day in July 1950. This road back to health was followed up with several more months of intensive rehabilitation in body and soul.

Regrettably, never having received any letters from Honey, and Honey not having sent anymore after she was mistakenly advised that Michael had been killed in action, he thought she had experienced second thoughts about their love, and had gone on to make a new life for herself not realizing it was only because she believed he was dead.

Two years later, in September 1952, Michael returned to the university in Wisconsin, carrying some scars on his body and many more in his mind and soul. But he was determined to pick up the pieces of his lost love, although he realized it had to be with the greatest of caution. He finished his undergraduate work, and with a bit of money he had saved in the interim, he decided to make a trip to Tennessee.

He did not intend to bother Honey even if he could find her. But to simply find out how she was doing and, perhaps get an answer to the ever burning question: What went wrong after he was sent to Korea? He retained a private investigator in Nashville to find out what he could as to where Honey might be and what her life was like at this time. The investigator nosed around Honey's small town near Mount Juliet, ostensibly trying to locate a Maureen McNeil (Honey's actual name), pretending that she might be an heir in an estate.

The investigator discovered that she was alive and well and living in Chicago with her husband and two toddler children. The investigator checked her out further and was told that Honey had married a couple of years after she lost a boyfriend in Korea. Everyone was aware that Honey had grieved a long time and then moved away from the small town because the memories were too difficult to cope with even among friends and family. Michael's love was a very personal and private chapter of her life that she didn't wish to share with anyone else any longer.

The investigator then went to Chicago and found everything to be as reported by the good folks in her hometown. Honey seemed to have married successfully and the marriage was as sucessful as it could be considering the great emotional pain that still endured when she thought of Michael, which was more than perhaps she should have after all this time. People who knew her reported that she appeared to be a particularly dedicated wife and mother. Her husband was a doctor, whom she met while he was in medical school at Duke University where Honey was working in the placement office. And after graduation, they married, and produced two children.

The investigator reported all of his findings to Michael, and the die was cast. He knew he couldn't call on Honey even though she was close to where he was living in Wisconsin. He now realized why she hadn't tried to contact him because she thought he was dead. All of his misgivings dropped away in an instant of understanding that she loved him dearly throughout. He was certain that, except for the terrible confusion about his wounds which she had believed were fatal, she would not have had to restructure her life and eventually take a husband - whom he hoped she loved - and become a mother.

He thought of driving down to Chicago and waiting along the street where Honey lived so he might be able to catch a glimpse of her as she came and went to or from her home in the daytime at which time he presumed her husband would be in his office, or at the hospital, or wherever else doctors are when not at home.

But after much internal debate, he vetoed the idea when he realized if he saw her, even for a moment, he could not restrain himself from going forward and speaking to her, which would scare the hell out of her, and would no doubt screw up her life, perhaps to a point of no return.

"Enough pain – enough pain," Michael said sadly as he died a little more inside. "I can't do this to her now. I love her too much." So he quietly bid a last farewell to his first and only love as he released her to her comfortable world where not knowing was much better than opening new wounds from which neither she, nor he, might ever recover. To love deeply is to understand the power of giving – unselfishly, unconditionally. Michael could only give everything he was to Honey by walking away and not corrupting her life.

"Enough pain. Enough pain," he repeated, and then turned his attention to whatever life would bring from that point on. He was determined to no longer look back with regret, but rather to look back fulfilled with the warm memory of eternal love he had tasted that very special, brief shining moment when they first became one in a little cabin on the edge of Junction City, Kansas. A love that was perfect in every way. And always would be. Which is why he was letting Honey go. Why he had to let her go.

******

Twenty years later, as Honey was browsing through the pages of *The Chicago Tribune*, her eye caught a headline and story about a Korean War hero who died saving a young child who had fallen on the tracks of an El train in the loop, and it was more than just a heroic account. Honey gasped as she caught the name of the man who saved the child. The man's name was the same as the soldier she met and fell in love with in Kansas many years before. The soldier who she thought had died in the Korean War. The article read:

WAR HERO DIES SAVING SMALL CHILD

Michael Malone, a highly decorated hero in the Korean War, jumped down to the tracks of the El to rescue a year old boy who had fallen from his mother's arms when she stumbled on the platform as the train was approaching. Malone was able to reach the child and safely push him back on the platform, but Malone was not able to scramble quickly enough up the platform before he was hit and killed by the train.

Malone had been awarded the Distinguished Service Cross, the Silver Star, and other medals for heroism in the early days of the Korean War in July 1950. During his heroic actions, which included charging a machine gun nest and putting it out of action, Malone was severely wounded the next day while saving another soldier during a brutal mortar attack and he was left for dead for many hours following the attack.

He was ultimately discovered to be alive, and after a long rehabilitation period, he returned to civilian life and went on to become an electrical engineer in Milwaukee, Wisconsin.

Malone was in Chicago attending an engineering convention when he met his death while once again displaying his heroic devotion to another in need.

******

Honey, who in Tennessee was known as Maureen McNeil, cried long and hard that day. Then she cut out the article, and sadly placed it in her old jewelry chest along with their letters from the past which she had sequestered in an antique trunk in the attic of her home.

Honey spoke to Michael feeling his spiritual presence in the attic beside her. "Michael, my dearest Michael, you left me many years ago in a war so terribly far away, and now you have been taken a second time. But now I understand at last why we never saw each other again after that wonderful night we fell in love and surrendered ourselves completely to each other. I am so sorry I never knew what really had happened to you. But you will never leave me again.

"And nothing will ever take you from me as you live forever in my heart. I love you. I will always love you, my first and dearest, enduring love."

Honey softly spoke these loving words to Michael and smiled in spite of tears that were falling softly from her beautiful eyes he had loved so much. And she felt him truly close to her in the secret world of her attic.

Then she warmly remembered that special time and place long ago in Junction City, Kansas, which seemed at that time to be - and always would be - the most wonderful place in the world.

The End

GOES EAST - COMES WEST

Not having made love to every woman I would have preferred, although loving more women than I should have, I conceitedly considered myself somewhat competent in the loving department. My conceit was misplaced. This is a story of how I painfully discovered that humbling truth. As I watched Sherii sleeping the sleep that good lovemaking produces, I immersed myself in the esthetics of her beauty while my male ego suggested - no - actually insisted is the better term, that her beauty was enhanced by my contribution to her contentment. Setting my male ego aside, if that were possible, I decided what was more important was my conviction that this time our involvement was right - now that I finally understood the depth and meaning of our relationship. As I studied her filled with love, an old English word, *wifman*, came to mind. It translates into: a woman who is a wife.

With Sherri there was a major technical difference, however. She wasn't my wife, or *wifman*, in the old English sense. She was someone else's wife. I didn't care. Confident that one day soon she would be exclusively mine, I was willing to wait. But if this was an accurate assessment, why was I troubled with more than a modicum of doubt about another man's wife and me? To dispel this insinuating hesitation, I reminded myself that I did not have to make any realistic assessment of our relationship at this moment, while at the same time, choosing optimistically to view her married status as a minor obstacle. Which could easily be remedied. And I was delighted she was sleeping next to me as she has been whenever possible for the past two years.

Sherri's loveliness was crowned by thick red hair covering the pillow and partly obscuring her face. Beautiful was an understatement, and while it would be disingenuous to suggest that she had no awareness of her exceptional beauty, she did keep it in proper perspective and did not appear affected by it. But I was deeply affected.

Looking at her was exhilarating, but ironically, it could also be frightening at times. The thrill of looking at her sometimes would be intruded upon by an irrational fear that suddenly all of this splendor would vanish without warning into that never world where so many things take flight when one holds on too desperately.

A short while earlier, before she fell into the very best kind of sleep, we had made passionate love. Perhaps the expression passionate love is a hackneyed redundancy. Isn't all lovemaking passionate? If it is not, then it cannot be making love, but rather it has to something substantially less. Screwing as a more gentle term than the “F” word might be more accurate. Which may mean that only one, or perhaps neither of the participants is enjoying the coupling aesthetically as well as physically. But even at that, it may not be all bad. As the old quip suggests, sex partners are all good; but some are better than others.

I had an old Marine friend who often reminded us, “Don’t bitch about sex pal, be happy you got it. Hell, the worst piece of ass I ever had was terrific, and it got better from there.” Wisdom from an old salt.

Tell it to the Marines.

In my life this sage advice found fruition a hundredfold. Making love to Sherri was not only passionate, it was lust filled, emotion filled, delicious, and, in the vernacular, just down right fucking fantastic. If it could be any better, I’d have to clone her and make two Sherris. Our loving was an act dedicated to body and soul, so intense it transcended definition. A kind of timeless rapture wherein she was mine alone caught in a universe without boundaries. I was confident she always would be. This time around.

But, regrettably, the rapture soon was intruded upon as an unwelcome alarm sounded a sort of post-coital wakeup call that bordered on sheer terror and replaced my giddy confidence. Was it possible, although I had to believe it was not probable, that she wasn't only mine, and could never be mine alone? Such terrible thoughts caused me to wonder how long this wonderful relationship could possibly last. She was with me now because we had renewed something that started thirteen years earlier when we first met. This was when we belonged to each other long before she married someone else. But time, and truly stupid decisions on my part, when we were both too young to know better, motivated us to part.

She later married a man of substantial wealth who wanted to buy and possess her as a beautiful showpiece. It was suggested by envious wags that this was his way of stroking an already over-bloated ego, but in truth his motivation was to possess Sherri as a trophy wife, and to misuse her as a vehicle to assuage a deeply disguised insecurity. It didn't take long, however, for Sherri to realize her primary status was more that of an obsessive object rather than a warm and loving partner in marriage.

This became fully apparent in her first year of tenure as a wife, and from there her resentment over being a prized possession grew quickly. As a result when we met again during the second year of her matrimonial facade, she was willing to resume the relationship we had abandoned many years earlier and to accommodate our needs, strongest of which seemed to be physical ones, even though she was married to someone else. In time those needs expanded, and her generosity was extended in mutual reciprocation of my filling her desire to be loved and wanting her solely for what and who she is, as it was when we were originally lovers, and not merely to function as a thing of beauty to placate the deficient psyche of her husband.

I was fully aware of why she was with me and was willing to immerse herself with no moral reservations. Was it right? Who cared? Did we feel guilty? I don't know if she did. I doubt it. I know I certainly didn't. I loved her fully and without reservation. What other rationalization was necessary? But yet it was frightening. Not of being caught. I could hand her husband his head in any confrontation, physical or otherwise. But frightening, nonetheless, because such intensity of emotion is not easy to handle.

People who claim they understand these things suggest that human beings are the only species capable of loving physically and emotionally at the same time. If this is true, it is a cursed blessing. More often than not, we are not able to fully engage in the joy of the present without indulging in foreboding. We tend to worry about how long this wondrous delight will survive rather than enjoying each other totally free from any other consideration. And then at the moment of high ecstasy we start down the long road of doubt, and fill our souls with anxiety as we tremble at the thought: Will it be like this next year? Or next month? Or even next week? Rushing to know the end right at the beginning is hardly a pattern for success. Caution perhaps, but not success.

Sherri, moderately tall at five feet seven inches, gorgeous of face and figure, presented no discernable imperfections, unless you consider a small beauty mark (translate: tiny mole) four inches above her right breast, a flaw. Whatever it might be considered, it was dwarfed in relative reference by its tiny size compared to her full breasts. This ravishing woman, now sleeping softly, was cradled in my left arm as I studied her. I thought I understood her completely since we had first known and loved each other many years ago. But it was all delusion. I could not understand her completely, and maybe not even more than a little.

Experience hard come by over the years taught me that the human female is an impossibly complex collage of heart, mind, body and soul, indispensable to the male human, but at the same time, truly mysterious beyond full definition. Sherri and I originally began as a couple back in my early days in Los Angeles when I moved here from Chicago to go to college fresh out of high school. We met on a train, the Santa Fe *El Capitan*, when each of us was seventeen. She was going out to visit her brother in Westwood and had planned only to stay for a few weeks. She stayed for two years because of me. Loving her seems a lifetime ago, but memories die slowly and my feelings ineluctably drifted into distant reminiscence in spite of trying not to allow this.

She too had just finished high school in Lake Forest, Illinois, when we met and shared, in delightful proximity, the entire 39 hours it took to travel by train from Chicago to the City of Angels. Inherently charming and with no pretense, Sherri, even then was genuinely unconcerned about her extraordinary beauty which had been molded by a bonding of fine Norwegian and Swedish genes that produced wonderful features and complemented them with a sensuous figure.

I loved her immediately. I was certain I always would. I was right. The passion had survived during the years we were apart, even after I was able to graduate from a state of perpetual, teenage protuberance. But thinking of her, as I did too often, never found me able to escape the breath stealing pain that memories of her produced. Especially when I recalled with aching heart how the bodies of Scandinavian girls and Irish boys fit together in a most delightful way.

I continued appraising Sherri as she slept and realized I had never been able to reason objectively about our relationship. But I was certain I had remained in love with her, not just in memory of the good times, but genuinely in love in the sense of wanting to give more to her than take from her. In my male, delusional self-importance, I was confident she felt the same about me. And, of course, I was certain we couldn't live without each other now that we were reunited, even if it only has been in stolen moments.

The only hitch was that we hadn't told her husband about this small detail. Although we never met, I didn't like him, and, naturally, to me he was a humongous jerk. But I had to admit he was extremely generous towards her and for some reason I chose not to denigrate him. It was enough that I was making love to Sherri. I didn't need to bad mouth the cuckold bastard at the same time. To this point in our deliciously, illicit affair, we had not discussed if and when we were going to tell him about us, after which she would make her break.

It never quite seemed the right time, but I assumed we would get around to it when it was appropriate after I was more secure in my professional life as an attorney. In spite of our putting off telling her husband what eventually needed to be told, I wasn't worried because my ego convincingly articulated that I was the only man she really needed or ever would. And yet, as I gazed at her, I wondered why I hadn't given more thought to approaching the subject that seriously required addressing sooner or later, and the sooner part appeared to be gaining on our procrastinations. Perhaps it was because I had asked myself many years earlier, did I let Sherri get away? Or did I push her away after our first two years together while I was in college. Until I could figure out what the hell motivated me to fuck up the best thing I had ever known, I had to admit I was afraid to jeopardize anything even close to that kind of mistake this time. We were only nineteen when I screwed everything up royally and lost her after those two fine years following our meeting on the train heading out to new adventures in Los Angeles. It had something to do with my inability, or at the very least, an unwillingness to make a life long commitment at that tender age no matter how good the loving. So we parted. Gut-wrenchingly parted.

And then we both tried to get on with the business of being whatever we thought we were destined to be. But only with great pain. It might not have been that difficult if we had met only once in our lives and parted somewhat early in the first few weeks. We were young and inexperienced. Blindly enjoying that wonderful time of life, when love, sex, and giddy feelings blend in a sweet confusion of mysterious grandeur and discovery. The sweet mystery of love is so often intermingled with the bitter mystery of life.

If we had separated early in the beginning, it would have hurt, but we would have realized that when young love doesn't work out, we don't have to kill ourselves. We could make the break and survive. And although we would remember the good times, we eventually would also understand that the maturational process of finding and then losing is so much a part of the youthful journey of learning, living and growing up. Nonetheless, at the same time we would painfully realize that no one ever comes away entirely whole from a genuine loving relationship. Not at any age. Some of you remains behind.

Philosophers contend that we grow from testing raw emotion in the fires of passion and we are enriched. I think they are wrong. Perhaps we grow in wisdom, but you leave part of yourself in the fires of love, and the missing parts plague like phantom limbs after amputation.

I can confirm most painfully how following our first two delightful years together, a great deal of me remained with the very special woman named Sherri, even though I tried to ease the pain with a succession of other lovely women. But I managed to stay single while making all kinds of impossible promises to them that created a host of disappointments without my wanting them to. Maybe I was looking for something that could never be. No doubt it was a reprise of my incurable malady of being in love with love.

True to my Irish nature, love seems to endure only when it ends tragically. It is an Irish form of self-destructive romanticism which suggests - that for love to remain forever, it must end in tears and heartbreak. I never could understand it. But I lived it. Time and again. The woeful tale of Juliet and her Romeo was more in keeping with my romantic instincts than fairy tale fantasies of happiness forever after.

During those intervening years, after parting from Sherri, I finished my first three years of college and then went off to war in Korea. A hard year and a half with the lst Marine Division, which included the invasion at Inchon in September 1950, and later the long fight back from the Chosin Reservoir, confirmed that Sherman was right, war is hell. But the Marine Corps made up for it by allowing me, after leaving Korea behind, to spend a couple of fine years in Japan with the 3d Marine Division at Middle Camp Fuji, located halfway up sacred Mount Fujiyama.

Once again I indulged in the pursuit of lovely women. This time Japanese. Slowly my sanity returned after the lunacy of war and I felt almost human again. Some of the ladies were brief encounters, some more frequent. But eventually, as if it were fated, a special person came into my life. And became a fixture in my heart and soul, who so very much like Sherri, can never be replaced in my eternal affection. Her name is Chieko.

I have no idea what Chieko stands for in Japanese, but if it has any meaning, it must translate into one who is a flower of extraordinary grace. She was a dancer in an all girl review in Yokohama, not far from Fujiyama. A showgirl, if you will. A Geisha in modern dress when she chose. But I loved her in traditional Japanese attire: kimono, obi, and getas. Actually I loved her best when she wore no clothing, but that came later. Which we discovered was the most appropriate way to rid ourselves of East vis-à-vis West distinctions.

Above all else, Chieko was gentle, loving, sensitive and guileless. I first saw her in a resplendent nightclub act in Yokohama where she was a principal dancer. I immediately decided she was a vision of Cio-Cio-San from Madama Butterfly. Only I didn't feel like Lieutenant Pinkerton, and truly convinced myself that I sure as hell would not have abandoned her if I had been in his position. Not even for Puccini. At one point in the show she appeared, almost imperceptibly, to have turned her head to look at me, and her eyes hesitated for a fleeting moment. Then they shifted away, not in rejection, but rather in that subtle Japanese way of not offending by either boldness or indifference.

She was dressed in a deep red and gold kimono, which enfolded her body in a concealing way so that I could not discern how shapely she might be without that colorful garment. But I was certain I wanted to know, and somehow I was going to know. The obi sash girdled her loins like a chastity belt, and it was obvious that my effort to know what she looked like, in what my old Irish aunt refers to as the altogether, was really going to take a lot more than simple seduction.

What I was most curious about was tightly guarded in her traditional costume, brilliant in color but terribly awkward in design. Nothing as facile as simply lifting a skirt and slipping off silky undergarments. My determination, which sprang more from sexual fantasy than good sense, should have realistically dissolved into an abandonment of the idea of seducing this lovely woman, but she was so captivating, I persisted.

As luck would have it, I was able to bribe my way into an introduction through one of the showroom hostesses, who was the girlfriend of another Marine officer. I wasted no time launching into a clumsy effort to ingratiate myself and asking Chieko to have dinner with me. She accepted, but only after what seemed like an eternity of silent consideration. And that was the easy part. The idea of sex was something quite apart. To be exact, we had seven dates before I was allowed even a brief goodnight kiss. Not an encouraging sign of more to come. But I pressed on, if for no other reason because she presented a worthy challenge. And besides, Chieko was gracious enough to laugh at my jokes, most of which were pretty bad, and she would hide her lovely smile behind her hand with the palm turned outward in that very feminine manner of a Japanese lady. Cultural traditions are hard to change. Even though this was 1953, and in spite of my protests and insistence, Chieko would walk behind me rather than next to me, following in the footsteps of male dominated protocol and subservience. All of which heightened the intriguing mystery of this very oriental lady.

In all, it took three months to convince her that it would be acceptable if we enjoyed each other body and soul. I was relying on a more universal connection in that context hoping that the cultural variances between East and West were not that different when two people wanted to know each other completely.

I later admitted to Chieko that frankly I had no idea how I had lasted that long without giving up in despair. Of course I didn't add that there is a mysticism that overwhelms the male ego when confronted with the power of perceived disinterest. Was it real or merely well calculated aloofness? I couldn't tell. Men are such easy marks for bright, beautiful women. And I could not let her go no matter how frustrated I may have been. Gratefully the wait proved worth it.

After we had finally consummated our relationship and established a most enjoyable sexual rapport, which quickly became emotionally enhanced, I asked Chieko why after such a long interval, she had allowed me to come to her in a complete way after resisting my many, not very subtle, efforts to take her to bed. She hesitated while looking directly at me with her alluring, dark eyes that seemed to hold a reserve I did not understand. I must have looked confused, but then her eyes misted over slightly, and throughout the pause, she held them steadily on mine. When she finally spoke, I realized it was from a depth of memory seared with great pain.

She told me of a young American Army officer she had loved when he was stationed in Japan in 1949 and part of 1950. When the war broke out in Korea, his sorely unprepared regiment had been called to arms in the early phases of that war, and he had been killed.

For a long time after she learned of his death, Chieko practiced the oriental custom of placing a bowl of rice before her dead lover's picture at each meal in memory of what they once had. It was an ancient rite that recalled a love that was lost, but in this ritualistic way could be forever shared. She stopped speaking and lowered her eyes for another moment. Then she turned back to me. I saw something new and deep as she softly continued, "But then you and I meet, and in time, I find two things. You very nice man. And picture can no eat rice." We never spoke of him again.

The war ended in Korea the summer of 1953. Having been rotated to Japan the year earlier, I wasn't in on the end when a truce was declared and only the formalities were left to be hammered out at Panmunjon, which locates on the border of North and South Korea just below the 38th parallel. The so-called United Nations police action ended like many wars do with some nominal winners, but mostly with both sides losing something emotional that can never be recaptured. Our side lost the innocence we believed we had regained through defeating tyranny in World War II. But Korea was still divided and our efforts were less than a smashing success in our pursuit of political solutions coming out of the barrel of a gun.

I didn't give a damn about international politics at that time, however, since I was immersed in my love affair with Chieko. I should add that politics on a national, not international, level were my ultimate goal, and as soon as my delightful odyssey in the land of the rising sun was over, I would be leaving active duty with the Corps and would head back to finish my final year of pre-law studies at UCLA, and then on to law school.

After which I would start on a long planned career in law and politics. But all that could wait as I finished my last year in Japan. A year of love and wonder with Chieko. We would take weekend trips to the many splendid cities and areas of Japan. She was particularly fond of the ancient capital of Kyoto, and autumn was her favorite time when we took to the wild, untamed hills that surround the city and we luxuriated in the rainbow of shifting colors, as the fall season seemed like it would extend into infinity. We hiked the trails that appeared haunted as they wound their way into cloud-filled gorges overflowing with timber, and then disappeared above the Takano River. We would stop frequently as Chieko prayed for both of us and her ancestors at many Buddhist temples and shrines that dotted the slopes and summits. These ancient, sacred places with their lanterns glowing at night cast a magical spell as the mists drifted between the many maple, pine and ginkgo trees, and revisited the spirits of thousands of years in that beautiful country.

Chieko reflected the quintessential Japanese woman in the tradition of millenniums of Nipponese culture. She was home in those mystical hills embracing Kyoto. The centuries old essence of that extraordinary city gratefully had been spared deliberately from destruction during World War II, which suggests that even in barbaric times wisdom and understanding can prevail. General Sherman certainly was right, about war as hell, and at times down right stupid, but not this time, and Koto was spared. It’s amazing how the human spirit can triumph over the pressures for vengeance.

I hadn't given any thought to what I would do about Chieko when it came time to leave Japan. But I knew I had to return to the United States when the Marine Corps said to saddle up and move out. I was painfully aware that I probably would not be returning to Japan except as a visitor. I couldn't live there. I was too American and too involved in my long range plans in law and politics.

This raised two serious questions: Do I take Chieko with me? Do I ask her to marry me? In one way the answers were easy, I didn't want to lose her as I had lost Sherri. But the solution was far from simple. Chieko was Oriental. I was Occidental. It has been suggested that East is East, and West is West, and never the twain shall meet, which has a nice ring, but actually is pure poetic nonsense. Many Oriental women left their countries and in time became thoroughly westernized, especially in America. Statistically, a majority of mixed East and West marriages have succeeded in fine fashion.

Chieko was different, however, and so was I. How could she fit into my long-range plans? How could I progress in politics with a Japanese wife, who would most certainly accommodate me, but who, unlike some women, would never truly be comfortable away from Japan? She would always be Japanese in her soul. And as a Buddhist, Christianity was out of the question. Also I knew, although ashamed to admit it, she would be a detriment to my plans. Maybe if I were in the Foreign Service, I could take a Japanese wife and spend years in Japan with the marriage as a definite asset. But my political ambitions were on a grander scale, and the early 1950's did not suggest that an accommodation of this kind would be a plus to my goals. So I put these thoughts on the back burner as we lovingly progressed through my last year in Japan.

We never spoke of my leaving. We never discussed marriage, or what the future might hold for us. Then, ineluctably, the day arrived when I got orders back to the States. I didn't mention anything about the orders to Chieko, although they were to be executed within a few weeks. Instead I went along with our normal routine right up to the day I had to leave, as if we were permanently bound in our love.

On the morning I was ordered to detach, I cleaned up and dressed to return to the base in the same manner I had for hundreds of mornings. Since I always left my uniforms at the base, I put on civilian clothes, but I took none of the other civilian items or personal things I kept at the house.

I tried to act as though this day was the same as every other. I held Chieko and kissed her and said goodbye in my usual, informal way. I did say *sayonara*, but rather I used a casual Japanese farewell gesture, *Ato deamisho*, that simply translated, see you later.

I didn't dare hold her too desperately because I might give myself away, so I limited my heartbreaking goodbye to a husbandly kiss and the pat on her tush I always performed when I would be gone only for the day.

I told her I would see her that night, but my beautiful Chieko, in her mysterious, oriental, womanly wisdom, saw right though me as if she herself had issued the orders for my return home. She looked at me with her soft eyes and demurred, "No you won't, my dearest love. I know you go home, and I never see you again. I understand your heart. I understand what you must do. *Sayonara, itsu made mo. Watakushiwa anatawa aimasu itsumo.* Loosely translated - Goodbye forever. I will love you always.

I protested, but my tears gave me away. I crushed her to me and kissed her with a sad passion. Then I tore myself away from her loving arms. As I walked down the path from our small Japanese home that gave me such comfort and welcome, I turned back for one final look at this gentlest of creatures. I waved, but I was too choked to speak. I never saw Chieko again, but I have her picture. Sometimes I put a bowl of rice in front of it.

*****

Four years later in the summer of 1958, I had finished law school and passed the California bar. I was working for a large law firm in

Los Angeles, and had finally embarked on my plan for a career in law and politics. On a flight to Chicago to take a deposition of a witness beyond the reach of subpoena, I thought how nice it would be to couple business with the pleasure of spending a little time with my family again. That plan didn't work out precisely as anticipated.

On that trip I saw Sherri after a nine-year absence. I didn't notice her when I boarded the flight. Too busy checking my seat assignment, I guess. But as things settled down and the plane was airborne, I looked around and for the first time realized that the beautiful redhead sitting across the aisle from me was Sherri. I stood up and said hello, apologizing for not realizing she was there when I first came aboard. She admitted she had seen me, but said nothing because she didn't know how I would respond. I asked the man who was sitting in her row on the aisle to switch seats with me. He readily agreed because I had a window seat.

Easing into the spot next to Sherri, I broke the ice by saying something goofy, but it was sufficient to push aside the nine years between our last time together, and they fell away as if they had been an illusion. I was irrevocably recaptured, not only in memory, but also by the same yearning and the same passion I had always known to fully possess this fabulous woman. I didn't say anything about this overwhelming desire at the time, of course, and we chatted like kids throughout the flight.

I discovered she was living in Los Angeles. Which I didn't know even though I had seen her picture on magazine covers and in many ads over the years. I somehow thought she had returned to live in Chicago, or perhaps New York, because she had moved onward and upward in the glamour world of modeling, gracing the covers of Vogue, Mademoiselle, and other publications dedicated to the female beautiful. She had evolved into an extraordinary woman and had become a model of substantial stature. I always thought of her as a great looking girl, but now she had blossomed into a truly smashing woman.

When we landed in Chicago, we made a date for the following night. She was there on a modeling assignment and would be free. Free to be with me, and free of her husband. We met for dinner at the Palmer House and I made no pretense about the sheer joy of being with her again. I blurted out, absolutely devoid of tact, that I realized she probably would turn me down flat, but I must say this anyway, "More than anything in the world, I want to make love to you, and you can now punch me in the nose if I'm that far out of line." And then, before she could reply, I suggested, hoping against all hope and common sense, "Lets adjourn to my room at the Morrison, or your room at your hotel."

To my delight and utter amazement she accepted my proposal, but thought it would be better if we took a room at the Palmer House where it was unlikely that she would run into anyone involved in her assignment, and we could enjoy anonymity. The food at the Palmer House was excellent as always, but the dessert that followed was even better, as we lost ourselves in a delicious reprise of sex and the kind of lovemaking we had delighted in before we parted nine years earlier. And we mutually sought to recapture the years we had lost. The next night we extended our lovely reunion, but this time we ordered room service instead of dining out. It was every bit as delicious.

After our return to Los Angeles we established a regular liaison at least once, and often twice, a week. It was easy for me since I was single, but Sherri had to finesse her absences for the most part, so we would meet in the afternoon at my apartment when she was ostensibly on assignment for the day. Added to this were some weekends when she was on modeling engagements back East. This is how we were for the following two years, and this brings us back to the present where she softly sleeps cradled in my arm after our loving interlude. Sherri stirred and opened her beautiful eyes. "How nice to see my big, strong Marine standing guard over me while I languish fulfilled with sexual contentment," she teased. "And I thank you kind, sir. I'd return the favor but you leave me so exhausted in the nicest way, I probably would nod off and fail terribly as a sentry. I understand that's a capital offense in the Marine Corps. Do you think a court-martial would convict me of loving a jarhead which I never thought was a crime?"

"I'd make an exception in your case. Probably reduce the penalty to a life of loving without possibility of parole. Think you could handle it?" I replied with a big grin.

"Yes sir, and if you are up for it so to speak, you can order the sentence executed right now," Sherri retorted with a taunting smile.

"I would, dear lady, but you'd only fall asleep again, and time has become of the essence. You have to be out of here in a little while, and I really have to talk about something now that we are in a relaxed mood. It's a topic which I admit is long overdue. But better late than never, and it's timely now because it coincides with an announcement I have been saving."

"Oh," Sherri replied a little apprehensively, more as a question than a statement.

"Okay," I continued. "No point in stretching it out. For openers I am changing firms. I am moving to a much larger one, only on the other side than I have been used to. My trial work now will be all criminal law and I will be with the good guys, so to speak. I have been offered, and I accepted, an appointment as a new deputy district attorney for Los Angeles County. This will be a departure from my usual mixed bag of civil litigation and criminal defense, but it is the foot in the door I need to pursue my political ambitions.

"Maybe five years with the D.A.'s office and I can get a state level judgeship. Probably municipal court first, and then superior court. At the same time I can work behind the political scenes the five years or so I will be in the D.A.'s office making a name for myself and then get a future shot, at not only a state judgeship, but perhaps even on the federal level, and then branch out into the possibility of national office, say the U.S. House or Senate. I have a lot of plans as I have mentioned in the past, and this is the first major step along the political path for me."

Sherri had started to dress and said nothing until I had finished my opening salvo. I watched her and felt the urge in my loins I always did when I saw her in various stages of dressing or undressing. I resisted taking her in my arms, and instead asked her how she felt about my professional changes, and what it might mean for us.

She hesitated for a few moments in order to sort out her thoughts and then inquired, "What do you mean by, for us, exactly? Do you mean to what extent would this change things, since obviously it possibly could? If this is what you mean, I can't answer that right now. I am happy for you if you want to leave private practice and take up the mantle of justice putting bad guys away. They should all be making little rocks out of big ones on some road gang or in a quarry. But your long-range goals may not be as financially rewarding as your potential in private practice indicates. By going into public service, you will always be limited financially to whatever the public is willing to pay for such dedication.

“Not that there is anything wrong with that, but it is limiting. And that brings me to the next part of your question. How does it affect us?"

"Well yes. That's precisely where I was headed," I answered. "That's what we really need to address."

"I'm not quite sure how to start on that question," Sherri volunteered tentatively.

"This comes as a surprise to me. I actually hadn't given any thought to such an abrupt change in your life, much less mine. I don't want to sound cruel in my reflection on this, and I certainly do not want to be cute or flippant. But this is suddenly a major issue.

“Perhaps I was being a bit obtuse in not seeing it coming, but we are going along so nicely, and I love the way we are, so I just didn't think about any changes. As sincerely as I can answer, I must say that if you are asking will this change our relationship, I would be less than candid if I didn't say the answer is yes and no. No, if we can keep things the way they are. But yes, if we can't. And by can't, I mean that if you are thinking of me leaving my husband and joining in your crusade, I won't do that.

“I am not saying this to be mean or deflate your noble ambitions. Quite frankly, joining you would be a step up aesthetically, but a whole bunch of steps down financially. I love you my gallant knight, but I am a specie of a sort of Darwinian financial evolution. I not only believe in the survival of the fittest, but most definitely, in the survival of the richest.

“So I have to ask myself. How I could abandon my current life style where I have the best of both worlds, my incredible lover who fills all of my emotional and physical and sexual needs and a husband who fills all of my many material needs, which I do not apologize for, not in any way, as crass as some people may think that sounds?” Sherri related this rhetorically but in a calm and non-accusatory tone.

I started to reclamor, but she held up her hand and asked to be allowed to proceed. "Tell me, when you are a deputy district attorney, just how much will the citizens of Los Angeles County pay you for your back breaking work on their behalf? Would it be enough to keep me shopping on Rodeo Drive every week? I don't intend any putdown by this, but I seriously doubt that it would be enough to allow me to shop there even once a year. And when you make judge or congressman or senator, how much will that put into our bank account? Which in all honesty means into my bank account? Your goals are lofty goals, but I do suspect they wouldn't produce much for my bank account because you are clearly the incarnation of the man Diogenes was looking for. Except for our affair, you really are the last honest man." Sherri said this softly without any sarcasm or any intent to patronize.

"Sweetheart, don't you see that we can have the best of everything by changing nothing. I will still be rich, and I know you won't ever ask for a penny from me because you are proud, stubborn and cannot be bought. But we can still have each other secretly and deliciously in this way. We have always been careful, and I suppose we would have to be even more circumspect after you become a servant of the public. But you know we will not want to give up our love and our truly wonderful lovemaking, so nothing has to change just because you are willing to make political judgments rather than pursue wealth."

"Wow, Sherri, I hadn't quite expected this sort of response. But I do appreciate your candor," I replied directly, but not angrily. "Only one question, is material comfort all that important? Hell, I'm not asking you to starve, but I will admit you would have to get by on a lot less if you divorced your husband, no matter how good the divorce settlement was, and take up legitimate housekeeping with me. Is that asking too much? I can't give you the Hope diamond, but I can give you a lifetime of unconditional love and devotion."

"I know that," Sherri answered genuinely. "And I am grateful for your love and dedication, but what you are asking is something totally foreign to me. It's like you were asking me to move to another country and adopt an entirely new lifestyle alien to that in which I have been immersed from the time you and I parted way back in 1949.

"Am I spoiled? Yes, I am! Could I move from a comfortable environment like a Japanese war bride who is asked to leave her familiar home and habits and assume a new identity and culture? I sense that really is what you are suggesting, but I wonder if you could truly expect me to do that. No doubt I should be embarrassed to say this, but I can't change that part of me that is so firmly ingrained. Maybe I sound terribly spoiled and perhaps even selfish. But that's who and what I am. And if you love me, you will understand that. Even though I love you deeply in return, I cannot change that part of me that truly requires comfort and security in mega doses."

Sherri then added, not letting me interrupt, "Like you, I am thirty years old and I make good money modeling, but this won't last forever. I require a whole lot more maintenance of life style than I could ever achieve even if I modeled until I was a hundred. So let's not change anything, and we can keep the best of both worlds for each of us, don't you see we can have each other and still pursue other needs professionally and financially."

I said nothing, and just looked at her beautiful face for perhaps longer than I might have under other circumstances, but I had to weigh carefully what Sherri was saying or I'd lose my control and blurt out something I would regret later. I finally responded. "Sherri, there is only one flaw in your otherwise reasonable argument, and it's a major flaw. The best of both worlds, of which you speak, is really only the best of your world. You have me, a devoted, willing and eager lover, and you have a husband, in name only, who provides you with all the goodies I can't, like wealth, unlimited comfort, and multimillion-dollar security.

"In short, you want for nothing. But how about me? How do I proceed in my professional pursuits as a single man who can't even bring you to professional functions. Especially on the next plateau which would be political functions. Do I lead a double life, assuming a private persona that brings us secretly together as soul and love mates, and then a public persona that has to date other women for purely professional show?

“Hell, I may as well just sign up with an escort service. Flashy broads for rent to cover my professional ass when it's show, but never tell. Damn it, Sherri, I want a wife, and even kids to flesh out my private and public life image. Not just the showpiece the guy you married uses you for. I want you as a real life lover, wife, and mother, to whom I can be fully devoted and about whom I can be justifiably proud.

“Damn it, how in the hell is what you are proposing the best of my world?"

"I don't know," Sherri answered frankly. “I only know what I am and how I need to have both you and all of my other comforts. I can't change. I will have to let you figure out how to manage that.

“I love you, but I can’t be anything except what I am. And you can’t take me out of my life style and make me happy, and I cannot accommodate your need for a tidy little family portrait to color your image in the public body politic. I'll leave the decision-making up to you, but it has to be on those terms. I'm sorry it has to be this way because I don't want to hurt you, and I don’t want to ever say goodbye again. You must understand, however, if you want me, you can have some of me, which is a whole lot more than my so-called husband ever had. And you can have most of me. But not all of me. There was a time many years ago before we foolishly parted that you could have had it all. But not now. I think even a little of us is better than none of us, don't you? I hope you will understand where we are and the point we cannot go beyond. Don't say anything now. Please just think about it and let me know. I'm sorry but now I have to leave. I cannot afford to be late."

"I know," I said sadly, "Oh God, how well I know."

Sherri just looked and said nothing, and then kissed me tenderly and left. I sat alone in my apartment wondering how in the hell I had missed the signals. I guess it was just a matter of letting time pass while having fun. But more to the point, it was a matter of avoiding questions I didn't want to confront, and failing to appreciate that, what goes round, comes round. Chieko's sad smile as I left her in Japan many years ago flashed before me, and I began to feel that there was no answer to this terrible Hobson's choice.

But, of course, there was.

The End

UNINTENDED CONSEQUENCES

This is a story about a highly charged lesson about life that began in war. I discovered after about ten minutes in combat that war teaches a great deal to those willing to learn. Those who aren't willing, are soon departed. Lesson one: War is a terrible thing. Lesson two: Kill the other guy before he kills you. You don't get much time to make up your mind. But this is not intended to be a war story. Rather it is a story of an additional lesson learned in a war - a poorly prosecuted war - and even more poorly understood. It began with the TET Offensive of 1968, in Hue City, South Vietnam. The Communists had taken the city. Marines, of which I was one, had orders to take her back. Life and death orders. Like we owned it or something. Like I gave a damn. But orders were orders. And the orders were to recapture this ancient capital of Nam and kill anybody who got in the way. I was nineteen years old. I followed orders and went to Hue. It was bloody, and some people might suggest that it was all part of the whole stupid Nam thing. But opinions differ on the specifics, and a consensus could not be found as a whole about that war. In the end it all came down for me, aside from the humor of men acting ridiculous under the stress of trying to stay alive, that doing dumb things was normal in Vietnam as I tried like hell to keep alive and kill those who were bent on killing me. The war in Nam gave a whole new meaning to the expression coined in World War II - SNAFU - "Situation Normal. All Fucked Up."

But I was told to go. I went. And I found myself outside of a Buddhist temple near the heart of Hue City. After inching cautiously towards that temple with my squad of Marines, I had expected to confront some suicidal Viet Cong (officially known as Viet Nam Cong San - Vietnamese Communists) and maybe some NVA (North Vietnamese Army regulars) to add to my personal killing list. Which list gave me serious misgivings about the wisdom of my being there at all even though I had volunteered along with a lot of other guys who hadn't exactly volunteered. But there were no Cong or NVA in the temple.

There was a monk, however, a sole and solitary figure sitting in that goofy way they sit when contemplating their navels or maybe meditating on the foolishness of people killing people. Hard to say which side was more offensive in Tet '68. The press had the

Communists winning, but the true facts later proved otherwise. We had kicked ass and the commies lost Tet '68. Although in ‘75, they won the whole ball of wax after U.S. forces pulled out in ‘71 and ‘72.

But at that moment in Hue City in February '68, it didn't matter who was winning, because the Marine Corps told me to jump and jump I did. Why? Well, nothing mysterious about it, I was a Marine. What else would I do? Sergeant Michael O'Shea, USMC. That's me. Still is, except for the sergeant part. I didn't need any better reason. And, in the process, I was learning a lot about living and dying. And later discovered that I still had a lot of learning to do about both of those serious matters long after I left Nam.

The monk hadn't looked at me as I trespassed on his sacred temple, although he had to know I was there. So I kept close watch to see if his intentions were something less than prayerful. I couldn't speak Vietnamese, except for the usual phrases which loosely translated into: Up with your hands, and get your ugly ass down on the deck before I ventilate you into your next reincarnation with more bullets than you can carry in your miserable gook body. Yeah, we called them gooks. Political correctness, an absurd creature waiting to be shoved down our throats by lunatic liberals in the good old USA almost thirty years later, hadn't crossed our minds in the sixties. Yes, I know. We were there to win the hearts and minds of the Vietnamese people. Yeah! Right! That's what we were told. But we figured that the best way to win their hearts and minds was to grab them by the balls and their hearts and minds were sure to follow.

It appeared that the goofy looking monk was not armed, and he didn't seem to be interested in harming us, so I softly apologized in English for invading his place of worship, and only then, as an after thought, asked him if he spoke English.

He acknowledged with a slight nod of his head that he did. I then asked him why he was sitting like a bent pretzel in the middle of all the hell going on around him, and he spoke for the first time.

"This is where I am supposed to be."

"Aren't you afraid?" I asked kind of stupid like.

"No," he answered.

"Why Not? I could have killed you just for being here and being a slope." He raised his eyes a little at the word slope, and quietly advised, "You do not offend me by your words, nor by your ability to kill me. You might kill my body, but you cannot kill the real person I am since in that sense I am indestructible."

"What the hell are you talking about? And by the way, how come you speak such good English?"

"Because it is what I had to do after the French left. I also speak French, Japanese and English. All the foreign invaders made this necessary. I do what is necessary."

"So why can't I kill you?"

"Because I am immortal. You can take my present form and destroy it, but I will live on, and if it is destined, I will return in yet another form as long as necessary to complete my personal cycle of causes and effects. I am eternal."

"I don't know what the hell you are talking about."

"It is not necessary," the priest/monk said softly.

“What’s that supposed to mean?”

I asked this wondering if I was going get to anything useful out of the monk. Obviously he wasn't going to give me any military intelligence, even if he had any to give. But he seemed like a wise old man, so I thought I would ask him a question. A sort of philosophical one. I had heard these guys were supposed to be some kind of philosophers.

"Can I ask you a question? It's something that has been bothering me for a long time."

As the priest paused for a moment, I wondered, what the hell am I doing suddenly becoming philosophical in the middle of intense combat. It's hard enough trying to figure out why I'm here, other than it was the only game in town. But, what the hell, I may as well ask the question that I have had on the back burner since first becoming a Marine whose mission I was taught from my first day in boot camp was to defend God and Country. And not necessarily in that order. My D.I. at Parris Island made it quite clear that I could give my soul to Jesus, but my ass belonged to the Corps, first and foremost.

"I would be privileged to answer any question you may have, if I am able," the priest replied gently.

"O.K., it goes something like this. Is there any force greater than love? I ask this because I thought I was in love a few times. But in the end, I discovered it was more lust and obsession than love. So I wonder why I keep looking for something that is actually elusive, although compelling at the same time?"

Not a bad question, I thought, but just one with probably many answers, like: survival, fear of dying, great sex pursued with total abandon, or the drive for power and control, to note just a few. But I hadn't any answers because love, or it's pursuit in my case, seemed to be the most powerful force I had experienced in my almost twenty years on earth. So I thought maybe the oracle in the temple could give me a leg up on this conundrum I had been playing mind games over for a couple of years.

He looked at me remaining silent for perhaps a minute, and then without patronizing, he replied, "It is the compelling force of responsibility."

"What does that mean?" I asked.

The monk calmly replied, "By this it is meant that one must leave himself open to act responsibly. That simply is, to do what is right in spite of every impulse and desire to do the opposite, or to refuse to act when you should. That response may not be as comfortable as love, but it is more compelling."

I looked at the holy man without any real understanding, and he added with a sort of fatherly compassion towards my apparent confusion, "Do not be concerned that you do not understand this right now. In time you will. You will know."

With that he resumed his meditating in the midst of the terrible noises of war and I didn't press him further. And I didn't kill him, even though I could have. Maybe, like he suggested, I was compelled to act responsibly for a change, or maybe I was just tired of killing people. Particularly people who belonged in Nam when I had serious questions about whether or not I did.

I thanked him with a wave, along with a shake of my head, which reflected I hadn't gotten his meaning, as I slowly edged out of the temple, and I resumed my personal war along with my platoon that had set up a perimeter defense around the temple. We remained in place for a few minutes and then, when directed by the platoon commander, we set out on a house to house effort to recapture Hue City, killing many Vietnamese in the process. It took more than three weeks to complete our deadly mission.

A few years later, having survived the nightmare of war, I finally came to appreciate what the priest meant as he softly and generously provided me with the real meaning of surrendering to the most compelling of choices of life while still exercising free will. Her name was Kelly and the forces of love and responsibility slammed together in a fashion that can be likened to an explosion of neutron stars.

Cataclysmic occurrences that give off more energy in fifteen second bursts of gamma rays than all the energy the sun will produce in ten billion years of its existence. I met Kelly in my first year of medical school in Chicago. She was twenty-two. I was twenty-four. She was beautiful. Comfortably tall at five feet eight inches, long brown hair, fiery green eyes, and a figure to die for. I had gotten out of the Corps after my Vietnam tour at age twenty upon completion of the remainder of my three-year enlistment, and immediately enrolled in college at Northwestern University in Evanston, Illinois. Four years of pre-med went well, and in my junior year I married a lovely girl from Wisconsin named Mary. After completing baccalaureate, I was accepted to medical school at Northwestern University in Chicago.

I was ready for medical school, but on the downside, I soon discovered was that I should have waited a few years longer before taking on a wife. Not that Mary wasn't a truly fine lady and totally devoted wife. She was that and then some. And I genuinely appreciated that she worked her buns off to get me through my last two years of undergrad and then into my study of medicine.

It was just that I was bogged down in sixteen hour days of studying, and between the stress of my professional aspirations and a devoted wife, who I couldn't - or perhaps it was that I wouldn't - share much time with any longer, marriage became more of a burden than I had anticipated or wanted. All of which made it unlikely as hell that I was going to get involved with another woman on a romantic level when I was already up to my ass in alligators while the swamp of daily demands was rising precariously close to nose level. But I did. In spite of it all. With Kelly.

It started rather simply. Kelly and I shared classes together, and we became part of a four-person study group; which kept us in closer proximity than I would have ordinarily preferred because Kelly enjoyed an earthy sensuality that attracted me and probably every other heterosexual male who spent more than ten seconds with her. But even though she was bright as hell, it wasn't just her brilliance and sexual lure that bothered me. It was, rather, that I was always hornier than the average bear, so I had been damn careful not to look for any sexual diversion from my already overwhelming life style.

Nonetheless, during lectures and study sessions I found myself sneaking side-glances at her, particularly at her lovely proportioned body, on top of which sat a beautiful head and face. I often thought what a delightful bedside manner she was going to project as a doctor, and it was certain she would attract a ton of patients - especially male types - who would be falling all over themselves just to be in her presence.

So I forced myself to keep her beauty and sensuality in perspective, and by working at it, I managed, not without difficulty, to keep my normal horny urges for Kelly under control. But just barely. I had to keep reminding myself that I was a married man, already late in starting the study of medicine because of my detour of three years in the Corps, and I had no illusions about what an affair could cost me. I was seemingly successful for the first two years of med school, with a whole lot of discipline, until one night a bunch of us med students went out to celebrate our last examination of the year before summer break. We went over to a local pub that was a favorite of ours, and I had more beer than I should have. I asked Kelly to dance to some slow tunes that were playing on a jukebox full of great records which gave off the kind of music where you hold the girl close. The owner of the pub, a World War II vet, had not emerged from the music of the forties, and he allowed no other on his jukebox.

I had never asked Kelly to dance before, and deep down I knew why. But after a few too many drinks, I refused to accept the reality that to hold her and move with heightening passion as I pressed against her would be dangerous at the very least and would break the dam of resistance against my hornier than horny lusting after her. Kelly readily accepted my invitation to dance, and I was hooked. We started with Glenn Miller's *Moonlight Serenade,* one of the most romantic songs of the forties. This led to Duke Ellington's *Mood Indigo*, and as if that wasn't enough of a passionate entrée, we then followed with a stimulating, lusty rendition of the tango, *Jealousy*, which dance was born in the brothels in Argentina; undoubtedly the most sensuous of all dances. All of which was a wonderful delight as temptation, bolstered by the sexually stimulating music, overcame reason and I was fully seduced by too much alcohol and the beautiful essence of the lady. So strong was the attraction, with inhibitions lessened by the devil's brew as the Irish priests used to say in prep school, that I kicked caution to the wind.

"You know, Kelly, if I weren't married, I'd be tempted to extend our anatomy studies to a hands-on exploration of the female body, especially yours. Now having said that, I am ready for you to bite my head off, and slap my face, and tell me to stop thinking with my phallus and get back to reality." I said this with mixed emotions expecting, but hoping otherwise, that she would rebuff my stupid advances generated by the strong desire to fully know her in a complete biblical sense. Mad desire exacerbated by too much alcohol and little attention paid to the potential consequences, is a euphemism for the old maxim: no man can reason with an erection, or to paraphrase, a stiff cock has no conscience.

"I wondered if you were ever going to admit how you felt," Kelly replied with a smile while pushing herself closer against me than I had already managed while dancing.

"Was I that obvious?" I asked naively.

"Something more than obvious. More like a sixteen year old male virgin in a whorehouse with a fist full of twenty dollar bills."

"Oh shit," I exclaimed. "I'm busted. And I thought I was being clever. Now I feel foolish, and I'm sorry I came on like that. Desire or not, it isn't what I had planned to do. Just sort of happened. I apologize. Jeez, I must look like a real jerk."

"Hold on, Michael. What are you apologizing for? For being human?" Kelly challenged. "Nothing to apologize for. I've wanted you pretty much the same as you wanted me. But I said nothing because you are married and I had resolved never to get involved with a married man. But I wavered in my resolve the longer I knew you. And now we both have come clean about our feelings. So what do we do about it?"

"Christ I don't know. Hell I never thought beyond the fantasy of making love to you. I always suspected that if I let myself go, I would look into your incredible eyes and tell you, as poetically as I could, that I wanted to fuck your brains out."

"Now that is poetic," Kelly said laughing, "something straight out of James Joyce. The Irish have such a way with words. And so my Mick friend, what would you do if I said I am willing to ignore all of the moral warning signs, and suggest we adjourn to my place since your place is clearly is out of bounds?"

"I would probably ask, before I lost my nerve and in spite of knowing better, how long will it take to say our goodbyes to the gang and pretend we are leaving to go off on our separate ways."

"O.K., then my place it is," Kelly said smiling at our not so clever ruse. "I'll leave first and wait for you at my car, which is in the med school lot. You know my car. I'll be sitting in it thinking of you and picturing your leaving the bar behind me after a respectable interval of not more than five minutes. I don't want to wait a minute longer. I suspect those will be the longest five minutes of our lives.

With that Kelly retrieved her purse from the bar and said goodnight to the gang. Just for show, I waved so long to her as she left, and then nursed the rest of a beer someone had bought me before I started dancing. After what felt like five hours instead of a few minutes, I announced I had to get going before my wife called and had me thrown out.

"Duty calls," I lied, as I bid my classmates a good summer and said I'd see them in the fall. I then headed for Kelly's car and we drove out to her place. She in her car, and I in mine. She lived on the near North Side of Chicago, and in a few minutes I was parked behind her in front of her house. We walked up the front stairs and stood on the porch for a minute before entering as I kissed her for the first time. It was better than I had imagined in all of my lust filled fantasies. We then exchanged several more kisses and held each other, understanding that the rest to follow was totally illicit. But we were over the edge and what else mattered at the moment.

So we savored the lovely, warm beginning of what promised to be much more than a mere romp in bed that would be nothing more than bim bam with a thank you ma'am at the end.

We moved into the house and left a trail of clothing from the front door to the bedroom, luxuriating in every lovely caress and taste. An hour later we lay still, exhausted and contented. Kelly, even more beautiful in her nakedness, leaned over me to turn on the radio which was set to an FM classical station, and then lay on top of me, her generous breasts fitting comfortably and temptingly on my chest. I spoke softly over the lovely strains of Rachmaninoff's Second Concerto, popularly known as *Full Moon and Empty Arms*, and said, "If you keep this up beautiful lady, I'm going to be obliged to start all over again."

"Is that a promise?"

"Yes," I said. And then did.

We fell asleep afterwards for the better part of an hour. When I awoke, I watched Kelly sleep the best kind of sleep. The sleep of the sexually contented. After a few minutes she opened her eyes, and said, "Oh you are doing what I wanted to do. To watch you sleep, knowing I put you in that wonderful condition."

"No problem. We can reprise that delight many more times if you will allow me, and then you can watch me sleep. I promise not to snore."

"You're on," she said with a lovely smile, and I wondered about the lack of guilt I knew I should be feeling at the moment. Kelly read the flash of expression on my face, and asked, "Something troubling you, Michael?"

"No, not really. And maybe that's more troubling than anything else."

"Oh?" Kelly replied as half expression, half question.

"Hey, don't get me wrong. You are the most magnificent woman I have ever known. I have no regrets and, for damn sure, no complaints. It's just that …"

"Just what?" Kelly asked hesitating.

"Oh, I don't know. It's just … I don't feel guilty and maybe I'm supposed to." "Oh, that. Well I don't either, and you are right, you should feel guilty. And so should I. But I don't either. So does that make us bad?"

"Bad is not word I could ever associate with you. You are not only beautiful, but a genuinely wonderful person, and if making love with someone you really want to be with is bad, no matter what their status, then so be it. I can't say I love you, but I know I could love you in time, and if we keep this up, I'm pretty certain I will fall in love with you. Maybe that's something I should be more worried about rather than not feeling guilty, but to tell you the truth I'm not."

"I'm not either, and to tell the truth back, I don't think I want to try and sort any of this out right now while I am feeling better than I have in my entire life," Kelly said sighing. I started to speak, but she put her finger to my lips and said to let her continue.

"I don't think I could say I love you at this moment either, but I can say you are very lovable and maybe I will fall in love with you whether or not you want me to. I am my own person. I don't give myself freely, and I don't ask anything from anyone who doesn't want to share himself with me. In that sense, I ask nothing of you that you don't want to give. I really love what we did tonight, and I don't give a serious damn right at the moment whether you are married or you are a Roman Catholic priest. I like you, and I truly loved what we did, and can do again, so to hell with any worries about the rest right now."

Kelly and I were on the same track, because I was feeling the same way, and I told her so. "I know where you are coming from and I'm with you. I know I could give you lot of jive about how I don't love my wife, or she doesn't understand me, or appreciate me, but it would be bullshit. I love her in my own way, and yes, I am very aware that she busts her ass putting me through school. So I can't say my attraction for you arises out of a lack of appreciation of her or any sort of diminished interest in her qualities. It's just that I too am my own person, and I wanted to make love to you from the moment I saw you. But I fought like hell to keep it a secret."

"Well, I'm glad you didn't, and I'm sure I won't need to get you half in the bag before you'll have the courage to seduce me in the future," Kelly said with a big grin.

"No fear about that. I just wanted you to know that I view myself as a man of character, but I must confess I have some chinks in my armor, and I wanted to know you completely in spite of, and not because of, anything I feel for Mary. That may sound a bit convoluted, but it's a fact. I know damn well if we continue to be lovers, I will fall in love with you, and then I will love two women at the same time. It won't be that I will necessarily stop loving my wife just because I love you. Some people think you can't love two persons in a romantic way at the same time. They foolishly limit themselves in this regard. I believe you can and I know I could. If that sounds crazy, so be it. It's how I feel."

Kelly said nothing, and I wondered if she was disappointed, but that was immediately resolved by her putting her mouth on mine and kissing me with such tenderness and feeling, I thought we might be going for thirds.

"I know exactly what you are talking about. I've been there and back. It has been almost three years since I had anyone to truly care about, Michael. Not that I haven't been hit on more times than I wanted, but there was no one after I lost someone special in a terrible accident. Someone I loved very much. You may be helping in the healing, I don't know. I only know I wanted to be with you in this way, and I was willing to look past your status as an obstacle after getting to know you over two years, and quite frankly, keeping a lid on my own desire for you. I might hasten to add, however, I think we now should continue this experiment in healing, or temptation, or whatever you want to call it, until such time as either one of us wants otherwise. O.K.?" Kelly said in a serious way.

"You bet your sweet ass. And I might add for the record, it really is sweet."

Kelly laughed and suggested maybe I should be heading back to the home corral since it was past the witching hour and I would have enough excuses to make without extending my absence on a night when med students didn't have to be studying for a change. I dressed and kissed her lingeringly.

"I'd rather be staying here, than going home. How's that for sounding the death knell on guilt?"

"Me too, darling. But you have to. That's just part of the relationship we have to live with. I thank you for tonight. Please know that I care about you. Goodnight. And call me tomorrow. After ten, however, since you have prepared me for a long, satisfied sleep. Drive carefully," she added as she kissed me quite passionately once again and eased me out the door.

I turned and looked at her one more time, and said, "I care too. A whole lot more than I realized."

*****

Kelly's place was revisited again and again over the next two years of medical school. Nights, afternoons, weekends, whenever we could steal the time. My excuse for being away from home so often was simple. Med school. Long hours of laboratory work along with study time in the library. Extra training at Chicago General Hospital, especially as a senior med student. But often more pretended than actually attended, as I alleged it had to be. So many reasons why I couldn't be home for dinner with Mary, and why I had to be working or studying on Saturdays and sometimes on Sundays. A million and one lies and excuses, and then more lies and excuses. But Mary accepted that I was driven by my ambition to succeed in medicine. Except, of course, for the times when my only ambition was to be with Kelly and do the things I should have been doing with Mary.

Not that I ignored all of my duties as a husband. I literally stole time from my stolen time to spend with Mary, and I made love to her in a dutiful, if not entirely passionate way. And my double life found the months and years passing quickly as Kelly and I moved inexorably towards graduation and on to internship.

I assumed Kelly was content with our relationship. It filled her needs while not interfering with her own ambitions and goals in medicine, in much the same way it filled mine. She accepted the fact that I couldn't be with her on those days reserved for families,

Christmas, Easter, Thanksgiving, and such, but I sensed it was difficult for her since her family was in California and she couldn't always get out there. Thus she spent some holidays either alone or with someone else's family.

Over time, in order to assure no resentment would creep in, I found myself spending less and less time with Mary and making more excuses so I could be with Kelly, which is what I actually wanted anyway. But a crack in our comfortable life style appeared the day Kelly and I found out which internships we had been accepted into. We had finished making wonderful love for the thousandth time, or so it seemed, and were lying peacefully in each other's arms when Kelly casually asked which internship I was considering. We both had been offered several potential opportunities at various hospitals, some out state, but only one of which was the same for each of us.

I genuinely wanted to intern where Kelly would be, but I had my sights set on a cardiac surgery residency following internship, and the one hospital where I had an offer, enjoyed the best heart surgery ranking in the country, and it was not the one where we each shared a common offer to intern. Kelly was interested in neurosurgery, which residency was best at a different hospital. I sadly answered her question to the effect that I would love to take my internship in the same hospital as she, but I felt I should accept the offer where a residency was more promising in the discipline I found most interesting.

I quickly added that I would want her to go with the best place for neurosurgery, because we could still be together even though not seeing each other everyday, as we had been fortunate enough to do over the past several years.

"I understand your reasoning, Michael, but I am suddenly terribly afraid of the prospect of not being with you on a regular basis. God, darling, not working with you will be terrible. What am I going to do without you everyday?"

"Well, let's see. For openers you'll miss me, and I'll miss you, and that we make our time together all the better," I answered teasingly. But it was the wrong time for humor.

"Oh? Is our time together getting dull? So it has to be better does it? So being apart is the answer is it?"

"Hey. I didn't mean that. It was a little humor to cheer you up. You know damn well that every minute I am away from you is like a day without air. Don't twist my words. It's just that we have professional goals which can best be served by taking our internships in the hospitals that accommodate those goals. I'm not about to give up what we have. I love you too much to ever do that, and that's all I'm talking about. We'll still be together, damn near everyday. I promise you."

"I know a better way," Kelly responded. "A way we can have the best of both worlds."

"Okay, what's this better way?"

"This is a little difficult to phrase because it makes me sound selfish. But what I am proposing is that you simply move out of your place, and into mine. I know this will lead to some legal complications, but surely they can be resolved. Maybe with a legal separation at first and later a divorce."

Kelly's proposal took me by such surprise I said nothing, so after a pregnant pause she continued, "Notice I didn't say anything about our getting married. That may be too much in the future, but living with you, even in sin as my old maid aunt would say, is better than living apart from you. So I want you to think about my proposal. You don't have to answer now. I know this is kind of a bombshell, and you will want to kick it around. So just think about it, and we won't discuss it any further right now. O.K.?"

"Okay," I said and closed my arms around her more tightly. It felt as if I might lose the thing I loved most in the world. "I love you," I said softly and sincerely. "I cannot imagine life without you. I'll think very hard about your proposal."

Later when I was leaving to go home, I took Kelly in my arms and with a heavy heart repeated my love and how impossible it would be to ever let go. She said she felt the same, and we stood holding each other for a long time without saying anything more. Then I kissed her with a heart full of more love, but also with more fear that something could harm that love, than I had ever known.

******

When I returned home just after midnight, I was surprised to find the front door unlocked, and although all the lights were on in the downstairs, Mary was not in any of the lower level rooms. So I went up to our bedroom and found her on the floor unconscious. I immediately checked for vital signs, and called for an ambulance and paramedics.

I attended Mary for shock and other distress waiting for the ambulance which arrived ten minutes late and we rushed her to Cook County General. Although she was only twenty-six, she apparently had suffered unknowingly for many years from a congenital cerebral aneurysm, which finally had ruptured without warning and resulted in a major subarachnoid hemorrhage flooding her brain.

Treatment, including surgery, was timely and life saving. But the prognosis was guarded and the potential for a lifetime disability was high because of a resulting stroke from the hemorrhage that had left Mary paralyzed on her right side, and, as later determined, twenty-five percent intellectually impaired.

I called Kelly and told her of the problem, and said I would have to put any decision-making on hold for a while until I could see what the final prognosis was on Mary. She was most generous in her sympathy and understanding, but I knew it was only a matter of time before I had to face the ultimate test of my love for, as well as my responsibility towards, each woman.

I saw Kelly a few times in the next two weeks, but passion was inexorably mingled with sadness and fear, and I knew I had reached the point of no return when the attending physicians advised that there was little chance of Mary recovering to anything near normal, and that she would require lifetime care and attention.

Fate had dealt an outrageous blow to Mary with unintended consequences for Kelly and me. I called Kelly and we met at her place to discuss courses of action. I was afraid to suggest anything that would tear us apart but Mary's condition added a frightful dimension.

"I am so sorry this happened to Mary, and to us, Michael. Particularly on the eve of our great hands-on adventure into the real practice of medicine. No more theory and hypotheticals. We are about to become interns, and we have a whole new world of learning ahead of us. I am so very sorry my darling. I know how hard you have worked."

It was interesting that Kelly had not addressed what this sudden tragic turn of events meant to our personal plans, but the message was clear. She was generous in avoiding the question, but it was obvious she needed an answer as to what road she should take in her own professional efforts, and it was decision time.

"I guess we need to come right to the point, darling. I owe you that much and more." Kelly started to speak, but I interrupted. "Please let me finish, or I'll lose my nerve and I will flounder in a morass of gutless retreat. Like we Marines used to say in combat, don't stand around with your finger up your ass, it'll get us all killed. Somebody do something, even if it's wrong. Inaction is more deadly than mistakes. So I have to grab the bull by the horns and wrestle with the dilemma Mary's condition has created."

"Okay, Michael. I understand, and I will let you start," Kelly answered a bit too calmly, while I was certain she wanted to rage against this disaster.

"Yeah. All right," I said sadly. "For openers let me say with all sincerity that I love you more than life itself. I would jump on a hand grenade before I would let anything hurt you. And yet now I find that I am the vehicle for more hurt than I could ever imagine. You need a decision about us, and I need to make it. What I must do, and I emphasize, must do as opposed to want to do, is to give you the freedom to make whatever choice is best for you.

"That is, the choice about your professional future without any interference from the fact that I love you so much I can't bear the pain."

As I said this and knowing that Kelly already realized where I was going with my heartbreaking speech, I saw tears well up in her beautiful eyes, but she remained silent and let me continue.

"About ten years ago in war I damned near killed a Buddhist monk in a temple in Vietnam. God must have stayed my hand because that very wise holy man taught me a lesson about life I didn't understand until now. It had to do with recognizing a force that is equal to, and perhaps even more compelling than love. He called it the compelling force of responsibility. Until a few days ago I didn't believe anything could be more compelling than my love for you. Now I know what he meant."

I paused because I was getting almost too choked to speak. Kelly just sat quietly looking into my eyes with more love than I ever thought possible. "It doesn't matter what my decision would have been to your proposition to move in together, and ultimately resolve my marriage status. But I suspect you know what the answer would have been if Mary hadn't been struck down by a potentially silent killer. I would have moved in and easily allowed our future to take a natural course. But all that is beside the point now, and whatever my answer might have been, the one that must be adopted now is that I have to set you free. Free to be yourself in every way because I cannot abandon my responsibility to Mary.

"In one sense it has nothing to do with love because I need to accept responsibility in spite of loving you in every way, and yet, at the same time, it has everything to do with love.

"I love you in a way so different than the way I love her that there is truly no comparison. They are different worlds. But in loving each of you, I have to sacrifice all of us. I have to wrench myself away from the splendor of the greatest love I have even known and let you go on with your life. And I have to die a little by doing so as I meet my responsibility to Mary. It is that compelling force that drives my decision. There isn't anything else I can say."

Kelly sat quietly for a long time. It seemed like a whole era was passing across my memory and then it fled out of sight. She finally spoke. No hysterics, no histrionics. Only a soft, "I understand, Michael. I know how much you love me, and how terrible this is for you as well as for me. But I would expect no less than this heartbreaking choice you have to make because you are who you are, no matter how much I would want you to do otherwise."

I wanted to reply, but couldn't. Instead I just sat there numb and softly crying as Kelly continued. "I was hoping against hope that this could be otherwise, but I knew deep inside that this is what you would tell me because it was what you had to do. So I called the Chief of Staff at Johns Hopkins Hospital in Baltimore this morning and said I would accept the intern position offered to me there," she said as tears ran slowly down her beautiful face.

"It would have been out of the question if this hadn't happened to Mary and we could have continued together here in Chicago," she added after a pause. "But I can't stay in Chicago now, as I know you will and must. This is where you have all of your roots. I'm from California, so I can migrate anywhere until I find what I want to call home. But not Chicago. Too many memories. Too much pain."

"When will you be leaving?" I asked, almost unable to mouth the words.

"In a few days. I'm sorry, but at least we can go on with our lives even though they are so torn up by this difficult ending to the greatest love of my life."

"Oh, no," I cried. "I could see it coming, but I hoped that somehow we could at least see each other. I knew you had the Johns

Hopkins offer, but I didn't want to believe you would leave Chicago. God! How can I manage without at least knowing you are close by?"

"You, will Michael. Just like you survived being wounded in war and coming home to a hostile crowd who didn't appreciate a damn thing you guys went through in Vietnam. You are a survivor, and I'll tell you something else, this will make you a better doctor. You are a first rate cutter; a gifted man with an innate talent for healing through surgery. You will be a great surgeon. And we both will survive, but in one way you are right, we will never be fully complete because part of each of us will die today. I'm sorry life has to be so cruel, but I respect your courage and for being a truly remarkable, responsible person. The holy monk was right. Someday you would understand. Now you do."

******

That was the last time I saw Kelly in twenty years, during which time we both prospered in our professional growth. I won the surgery residency I coveted, and she went on to neurosurgery and became well known in the field in San Francisco where she returned after finishing several years of study at Johns Hopkins.

Mary never recovered enough from her trauma to be self-sufficient, but her mother, a saintly widow, moved into our apartment when I was in internship and residency. Mary was never left alone. When I wasn't at the hospital in training, I would spend most of my time with her, something I did so little of when she was well. Fate deals strange hands. This was mine. But I didn't resent her for a moment. In fact I grew to love her more as the years went by, while never for an instant forgetting Kelly and the intense love for her that had burned so deeply into my soul.

A few days ago I read in the Medical School Alumni News that Kelly was now teaching at Stanford Medical School, as well as recognized as major practitioner of neurosurgery. The item also noted that Kelly was presenting a paper at the annual meeting of the American Medical Association slated to be held in Chicago in a few weeks. The paper was on recent techniques in the resolution of the kind of brain trauma that had affected Mary, and all of our lives. The new technique, if known then, might have made a major difference, but that was twenty years ago. I had kept up with Kelly's professional accomplishments, principally through occasionally making inquires of friends, but I never called her, nor intruded in her new life.

I thought it would be quietly nice, however, to see how well she had turned out after all these years, so I decided to be in the audience when she delivered her talk. I sat in the center of the auditorium so she would not see me, but the location still gave me an opportunity to watch her carefully. She hadn't changed much. Her long brown hair was cut shorter, but it was still rich and shiny, and her forty-seven years of life had not diminished her beauty a bit, including her lush figure that men would still kill to possess. It was as if time had stood still for this extraordinary woman, and I was genuinely moved by seeing her.

She also seemed to have developed an air of professionalism that gave her an appearance of greater strength and confidence. I could see why she was an unqualified success. And yet while pausing from time to time as she delivered her address, she looked directly at the audience of doctors who could not help being captivated by her beauty. It was then that I detected something perhaps only I would know. There was the slight touch of sadness to her otherwise fiery green eyes as she gazed at her colleagues and seemed to silently ask if, in spite of her many accomplishments, they thought her physical appearance was the most important part of what she truly was.

I knew that look, because I knew her vulnerability. Something she had steadfastly refused to reveal to a difficult world of demanding professionals. And I knew only too well the sadness that was showing in her eyes. I last saw it twenty years ago, the day we each died a little.

After Kelly finished her presentation, for which she received a long and genuine applause from her peers, I resisted the temptation to go forward and say hello. I didn't leave the auditorium right away, however. I just sat there watching her answer a few questions from people who had proceeded to the stage while others were filing out. After everyone had left, except her escort from the AMA, Kelly gathered up her notes and turned to exit the auditorium which would take her directly past where I had remained sitting longer than intended. I knew I had lingered so I could keep looking at her and savor the feelings that had never deserted my heart and memory. As she came down the aisle, I got up and tried to leave before she reached the row where I had been sitting. But I was too late.

"Michael?" she called somewhat startled. "Is it really you? I can't believe it."

"Yes, it's me. I didn't want to intrude and had planned to leave before you could know I was here. But I never could resist you, and there was no way I could give up even a few more minutes of seeing you. I think deep down I wanted you to catch me playing this silly game."

Kelly's escort, sensing that this was clearly a very personal situation, said she would meet her in the lobby to finish up a couple of administrative details, and say goodbye. After the escort left, Kelly looked at me with something more than surprise and curiosity. "I'm flattered," she said. "Thank you. I thought how difficult it might be to come back to Chicago, but I convinced myself I would not look you up because it would only renew the hurt I tried to bury all these years. Now you have solved that for me, and I am happy to see you. So how have you been?" she asked smiling in her beautiful way and reflecting a genuine pleasure in seeing me.

“O.K., I guess. I’m doing what I wanted to do in medicine. And while not as well known as you, I've had a modicum of success."

"A modicum," Kelly laughed. "Such humility. You are considered to be one of the finest cardiac surgeons in Chicago. A modicum of success indeed. You see I kept up on you too."

"God, it's good to see you, Kelly. I'm sorry if this will be a problem for you. The last time we said goodbye was the worst moment I have ever known, and ever will. I wouldn't want to open old wounds."

"Thank you, Michael, but it's all right. We both know you did what was right and I truly respect you for that. By the way, how is Mary doing?"

I paused for a moment and then softly replied, "Mary died two months ago, but thanks for asking. She fought the good fight. But it was too much for her. I think she willed herself to die. Her failing heart had been weakened by the long stress of the stroke and her inability to be the person she was before she was struck down. I couldn't do anything to cure her. In spite of all my encouragement and moral support, she lost the will to live, and she welcomed death as she passed on quietly one night in her sleep. I buried her and the last chapter closed on a long story about love and responsibility."

"I'm sorry, Michael. Oh God, I'm so sorry. You've had so much pain."

"I'll be all right, Kelly. Life goes on. But some things never change."

"Like what?" Kelly asked, her flashing eyes wide with curiosity.

"Like my love for you. It never changed."

“I know. I’ve been there too,” she answered a bit sadly. But then Kelly brightened and sassily asked, "Did you ever wonder if I married or what I was doing outside of medicine?"

"Or sure, but I never heard much about your personal life, only your professional life. I had a couple of spies who would brief me on your doings now and then. But never heard about a husband or anyone else though."

"That's because I never married. You want to know why? I'll tell you even if you don't want to know," she laughed. "I had several proposals, and some limited relationships, which I kept deliberately limited, but I never met anyone who could compare to you, so I refused to compromise. Don't let this go to your head, but once you've had the best … Well you know the rest."

"You are really free then? With no commitments?" I asked with undisguised enthusiasm.

"Yep! Really free and with no strings," she replied with a warm smile. "Want to go to dinner and talk about this. Maybe we could make it a little like in the great movie, *Casablanca*, where Rick tells

Louie that this just might be the beginning of a beautiful friendship. And, in our case, maybe a whole lot more," Kelly teased while displaying her lovely smile once again.

"Yeah, sure. You bet. Let's go over to the Palmer House," I replied, hardly able to contain my mounting joy. Kelly looked at me in the way she did that night in the pub when we had just finished our second year in med school and we embarked on a magnificent love affair, bringing back a flood of warm memories.

Then she reached for my hand and asked, “You want to kiss me now, or do I have to do all the work? I still love you, you big Mick. It surely would take more than twenty years to put even a small dent in those feelings. Certainly that shouldn’t come as a surprise."

I couldn’t think of anything in the world I wanted to do more right at the moment. So I did. We kissed passionately and twenty years fell away as if it were only yesterday.

The End

THE KISS OF DEATH

Catlin and Mickey. Perfectly suited. A handsome couple. Well, Mickey was ruggedly handsome. The kind of guy who made women wonder if he would be a gentle lover even though he presented an almost too strong an appearance; the kind that deceptively suggested arrogantly, macho, good looks.

Catlin, on the other hand, had a delicate beauty, which in itself was deceptive, because she could be as tough as Mickey when things got sticky and someone was trying to get her to do something she didn't want to do.

But the handsome couple, for want of a better description that doesn't suggest a cliché, were professedly very much in love. And in truth they were, and had been for a long time. So it was going to be a big wedding. The third one for each of them. Minister, ballroom, orchestra, great food, lots of booze and bubbly, and several hundred friends. The wedding to end all weddings. And everyone who mattered, at least to Mickey and Catlin, was there. Everyone, that is, except Catlin and Mickey.

Neither of them showed. And neither knew at that moment that each had made his and her bird. At the moment she was supposed to be gliding down the aisle to the traditional strains of here comes the bride (she had a lot of practice in that department), Catlin was sitting in a motel near San Francisco International Airport, thinking about flying off to the land down under, aka, Australia but she didn't have her passport. So she decided to do something she would have to do sooner or later in any event. And she wrote a letter of apology to Mickey explaining the why and wherefore that made her jump ship and not show up for the nuptials. Mickey, ironically at the same time, was sitting in one of his favorite watering holes in the North Beach area of San Francisco doing the same thing. He had started at the Buena Vista by belting down a couple of Irish Whiskeys, having passed on the famous Irish Coffee for which that special bar was noted.

Neither of the intended participants in the wedding of their lives (well one of the weddings anyway) thought to call the hotel management and tell the good folks who had all the preparations ready for them, that it was perfectly all right to go ahead with all the fun and stuff except for the actual exchanging of vows. But, when neither the bride nor groom showed up for the ceremony and more than an hour had passed, one of the brighter guests had the good sense to ask the manager of the hotel if all of the very expensive preparations had been paid for in advance. And, if so, he suggested that rather than arm wrestle later on with the mysteriously missing host and hostess, why not just break open the champagne and have the reception anyway?

"Hell, nobody really gives a damn whether the bride and groom are here," the guest sagely observed. "Actually aren't they merely window dressing for the main reason why most people go to weddings. Which is why all the freeloaders come to party to begin with. They don't really give a damn whether or not the dumb couple is there as the moochers secretly give thanks they weren't the poor suckers who decided to tie the hangman's knot."

The manager saw the wisdom of this logic, and not wanting to hassle over a refund for the missing couple, he told the orchestra leader to start the music and he directed the waiters and waitresses to move along with the dinner as if everything were according to plan. A great time then was had by all, except Catlin and Mickey, 'cause they weren't there. But it was better that way.

In her letter Catlin asked Mickey not to hate her for disappointing him by running out at the last minute. She said she loved him dearly and the only reason she didn't show up was because she had tried marriage twice before, and each time it turned out to be a very bad decision. Her emphasis was on a precipitous loss of sexual interest - not in sex itself - but in sex with the guys she married.

She wrote quite truthfully, "It was always good before the ceremony, but not so good after, and in time, just plain lousy. I discovered that a guaranteed cure for romance was to get married. I just could not risk it again, Mickey, not even with you. Or maybe it was especially because of you. Sex with you and me is so absolutely magnificent, that I wouldn't want something as formal, legal, and terribly, God awful, smothering as marriage can be, to interfere.

"It was always good with us, especially when we were married to other people and we weren't supposed to be messing around under the sheets. Which for me was always the best. If I'm not supposed to being doing it with anyone except my husband, in truth I enjoy it the most when I am fooling around. Nothing like the forbidden fruit, hey my Irish love? Maybe I am different, but I think it's only that I admit to feelings most other people only internalize and pretend don't exist.

Please understand dear Mickey. I do love you, and if you can ever forgive me, maybe we can have a reunion of sorts, and screw our brains out without any of the pressure to conform to conventional mores that mandate we are supposed to legalize our passionate responses. Which is the last thing I am interested in because it is so goddamn mundane. I love you. Call me if you ever get over wanting to kill me."

Mickey, of course, hadn't known Catlin had chosen not to show up, nor had he received her explanatory note, as yet. But he felt he ought to let Catlin know why he hadn't appeared at the big event, believing that she had. So after his third Irish belt, he took pen in hand. On the blank back of a menu he penned pretty much the same apology that Catlin had written, relating regrets and his reasons for leaving the blushing bride at the altar. People who screw wonderfully together soon begin to think alike.

"Better now than later, Catlin, dearest. I would only hurt you in the long run, because I believe that the greatest sex I have ever known would go south if we got married and took all the edge off of it. Then where would I be? I'll tell you where. I'd be out shagging ass all over the place. And that wouldn't be fair to you. You would only end up getting hurt.

"So please forgive me, and if you ever get to the point where you don't want to castrate me, call me and I'll come flying back to your arms, your big, wonderful, succulent breasts, your lovely legs that wrap around me so tightly, and everything else in between that is so marvelous about you. And not to forget, your fine mind too. You have a great mind, which is perfectly situated in such a way that I always want to get into your head. Ha! Ha!"

They mailed their respective letters to each other's addresses, which they were going to abandon after they set up housekeeping as husband and wife. And they each received them at the same time. So the epiphany was complete as they realized, for the first time, they had run out on each other. And, of course, they were pissed. It's O.K. to leave someone at the altar, but not O.K. for that someone to leave the other someone with his or her finger up his or her … well, let's say nose for want of a less gentile word. And then bug out.

After the being pissed phase had passed, however, and the humor, as well as the wisdom of their double flight from trouble had sunk in, they each laughed and rushed to the phone to call the other.

"Catlin, this is Mickey. Got your letter. You are absolutely right. I said pretty much the same in my note. Did you get it?"

"Yes, I did, Mickey. Wow, what a surprise. I thought I was the only one being a real shit. Well welcome to the club, but at least we made a valiant attempt not to fall into the buzz saw of marriage. Talk about luck. And hey, no hard feelings. I still love the hell out of you, and miss you something fierce."

"Me too, Catlin. What a narrow escape. Could have screwed up all of our great screwing. Incidentally, want to get together? Your place or mine, and we'll celebrate our narrow escape from the kiss of death."

"Sounds great Mickey. Let's make it mine. I'm going to take a nice long bath and get myself all smelly good for you. See you in about an hour."

"I'll be there. Up and ready, my darling."

*****

And so, once upon a time, two very sensible people found love and enduring romance by focusing on the golden rule of marriage avoidance, to wit, familiarity breeds contempt. But eventually they did marry, not because they thought it might screw things up between them. Oh, no. They simply married for other reasons.

Catlin did it for money. She married a fairly decent guy, but he had no real sense of humor. And for the money she allowed him to bang her ritually as often as he wanted, but she never did it for fun for herself. Faking orgasms to stroke his ego was easy because Catlin knew what the real ones were truly like. She and Mickey had shared so many of them. And her performances, enhanced by the right amount of heavy breathing groans, paid off in a ton of material comforts.

Mickey equally married for selfish reasons because his professional and social life required him to finally have a wife to take care of showcasing his potential for advancement in the world of corporate success. The, not so lucky, lady was the daughter of the corporation's largest shareholder. A trophy wife who was socially stacked, and full of all the graces necessary to carry him along the road to CEO of the big business. He perfunctorily screwed his wife pretty much like he used to screw whores when he was in the army. No foreplay, no after play, just bang, bang, and roll over. The trophy wife pretended she didn't care. But after two years of really lackadaisical humping, she got a full time lover on the side. She had it all then. Money up the ying yang, and hot sex twice a week with her stud, whom she kept in grand style with all the bucks she fleeced out of the ambitious Mickey.

Mickey knew all about it, but didn't give a damn. He thought it was funny, and he didn't have to perform much just for show with his cheating wife. Really funny.

The real key to Mickey's and Catlin's enduring relationship, however, was not this diversion through marriages of convenience. Rather, it was that the great sex they had always enjoyed with each other. This was the glue. Thus the sham marriages to their respective spouses were not a hindrance. Conversely, these marriages of convenience were a help in their enjoyment of great sex outside of marriage. How interesting that, in this paradoxical way, their marriages were never considered an obstacle. They saw them as a safe harbor wherein they could ride on the smooth waters of ecstasy without thinking about doing something really dumb, like getting divorced and marrying each other. In this wonderful, ironically, perverse way, their marriage facades were an absolute boon to their extracurricular sex adventures. So they just went along full of caring and joy as they regularly screwed each other like a couple of horny rabbits as often as possible; sometimes as much as three times a week. Which is more than some of their married friends did in a year. In this fashion their amazing affair lasted twenty-five years because the sex never got bogged down in legitimacy. And they lived happily ever after.

Well almost ever after, except for one unexpected event. It appears that Catlin's conservative, no-nonsense, no sense of humor husband, clearly could never fathom, no matter how much he might try if he knew about the long affair, the depths of the habits of the heart and genitalia that had inextricably bound Catlin and Mickey rolling in the hay together. Bad form really for this selfish guy, totally devoid of noblesse oblige.

The “hay” in this instance was the cuckold husband’s bed, in his home, at a time he was supposed to be out of town. Catlin loved to ball with Mickey in her husband's bed. It was so deliciously wicked. But Catlin’s husband, who had no sense of humor, much less a modicum of understanding, snuffed Mickey where he lay. It was done with a .45 caliber round to Mickey's head, which head Mickey had just been using to address Catlin's golden valley.

At the moment of Catlin's coming, Mickey realized that he might be going. So in his wonderful Irish way, when staring tragedy in the face (Oh how the Irish love that moment), he summoned up his Irish wit and suggested to the asshole who was about to dispatch him from the planet, "Lighten up, Lad, you know the old saying, eatin' ain't cheatin'."

The asshole didn't smile as he squeezed the trigger. Such a terrible waste. It was quite a scandal, of course, but everyone who saw Mickey at the lying in would swear he had a smile on his face.

Catlin divorced her husband after he was convicted of a serious degree of unkind homicide and sentenced to many years behind the walls in a California state prison to make little rocks out of big ones.

Catlin then took all of her convict husband's money and moved to the French Riviera where she kept a stable of young studs who came and went. Literally. And she was perfectly content. Well almost perfectly, since she did miss Mickey. Sometimes more than she wanted to. Great, forbidden, sex is indelibly imprinted on the memory.

Funny when you think about it. Catlin and Mickey had dodged the kiss of death that marriage to each other would have been, but the fatal kiss that ultimately ended their sexually great and delightfully, illicit romance, that had endured for all those years simply because it was not supposed to be happening at all, was the fatal bullet that kissed Mickey's brain, which missile had been illegally sent his way by Catlin's husband. Which is the only reason their very special love affair finally came to rest.

Some guys, like Catlin's convict husband, who are devoid of humor and compassion, clearly do not appreciate the magnitude of how great a love can be when a man and woman really love deep down what they are doing - with - and to - each other.

The dumb, stupid, cuckold bastard had no sense of humor and obviously not an ounce of empathy or grace.

Sure is funny.

The End

LOVE LETTERS

15 April 1968

Dearest Cynthia,

Some nut once wrote that everything changes so it can remain the same. Whatever that is supposed to mean. Sounds like unadulterated bullshit to me. Because everything changes. And when the changes come, nothing remains the same. Or maybe you would prefer Thoreau's take on the subject after a year of solitude in the woods on his own golden pond when he wrote, "Things do not change; we change."

So take your pick, it's not essential. What really counts is that we either evolve, or we die. And this includes my love for you. O.K., just hold the laughter. I'm serious, and, damn it, this is supposed to be a love letter. So believe me when I say I've changed, and my love for you has changed too; only it's for the better. Of course that doesn't do me a damn bit of good if I can't express it like I used to in the old days; even before it got better. And why's that? Because you got married while I got to go to Nam to get my ass shot off in a war no one has successfully explained to me or anyone else.

Now, as I recover from my wounds, I am reposing not too comfortably in the Naval Hospital in Da Nang, South Vietnam. Da Nang used to be known as the Paris of the East, but now it's more like the rear end of the universe because the "gooks" came out of their bamboo to celebrate their version of New Year, a.k.a., "Tet '68."

I could live with my current run of bad luck, but it's not all bad I guess since I'm still alive and I still can get my schwantz to stand at attention. But the bad part is centered on the fact that you got married, which you warned me you were going to do if I didn't get my act together. Which, of course, I didn't. And you lived up to your word.

So much for those wonderful times along the lake where we picnicked a whole lot. I thought they counted for something. Remember those lovely days? I do. And I can still hear the birds singing sweetly as we screwed our brains out on the cool grass hidden in a secluded glen under dense trees. When the blood wasn't blasting out of my brain on its way to parts somewhat lower, that is. All of which made our loving even more delightful.

But that's changed now, and I don't know what the hell I can do about it. I thought maybe if I wrote and told you how I am sorry as hell that I screwed up and I went off to this strange land without so much as a "please wait until I get back, and I'll do the right thing when I do," that you would understand and we could get back to things the way they were before I really goofed.

O.K. I know I blew it, but it wasn't because I didn't want to commit. It's just that I was a coward about commitment. A conscientious objector when it came to promising forever. Which made me a devout coward I guess.

But coward or not, I want you to know that I love you, and I don't give a damn if you belong, only somewhat I hope, to someone else. And I am damn sure, … (ugh, I can't even say his name) doesn't own you completely, because part of you will always be mine.

I know it. And you know it. So that's why I am writing you in care of our mutual friend, Terry. I hope you will write back, because I am really on a downer and maybe, just maybe, we can make something work to lift my spirits, and a whole lot of other things too.

Now I'm not suggesting you leave your husband right away. At least not until you finish this letter. Sounds asinine, I know, but it's just that I also know you will get tired of him after a while, because he isn't me, and never will be. I realize this sounds pretty cocky, but that's just the way it is. And so I figure if we can stay close through letters, I will have a fighting chance to make up for my stupidity when you finally dump the jerk and give me another shot at trying to do things right.

What I am trying to say my love is that now I am convinced everything really does change. And not so it can remain the same. But so that it can be better. Jeez, what a ridiculous concept the alternative is. Such crap, that everything changes so it can remain the same. Jeez, who thinks up that shit?

Now when I speak of change, this includes you, because I know you will realize that being married to him and not to me is something sorely in need of change. I keep thinking about those lovely picnics and the cool breeze on our nakedness when we made love with reckless abandon among the trees and tasted every inch of each other in a glorious passion. God! How I remember your beautiful breasts. And that was just for openers. I passionately remember everything we did, and everything about you that I did. Ha, Ha.

O.K., enough of this horny reprise. More in my next missive. But I beg you to think about it and then write me back. I miss you so goddamn much I ache all over. I love you, believe it or not, and I am sorry I seriously messed everything up.

'Till next time.

All my love,

Danny

******

April 22, 1968

Dear Danny,

Terry delivered your surprise letter yesterday. You sent it a week ago, and that's pretty fast coming from Vietnam. What a shocker. I never expected to hear from you after you found out I had married Colm. By the way, that is his name. The name you couldn't even say in your letter.

Really Danny. Get a life! Yes, I am married, so that's the first thing you must come to terms with. And, of course, there are other things too. So where to begin. Let's see.

Yes, at first, I missed you terribly. And I missed the good things about our relationship, but definitely not the crummy things. But then I found Colm. I mean truly discovered him. And I want you to know that he is a brilliant and terrific man; who is also very sweet. I imagine you will choke on reading that. But I have to be honest about my former feelings for you, and my present, genuine appreciation of him. The comparisons are easy to make, of course. He treats me like a queen. You treated me like a peasant.

You had met Colm once, very briefly in person. But I know you heard a lot about him from others; which comments you pretended to ignore. You and he met in a restaurant. Remember Coco's, the Italian place with a terrific wine cellar? He was there with someone who could have played Mariam the librarian in *Music Man.* Colm worked down the hall from me at the physics research lab at IBM.

Maybe you don't remember, or don't want to. He holds a Ph.D. in physics from Princeton. Pretty smart guy. In any event, Colm and I started dating after you made it clear that you and I would have to put a whole lot of time between what was then and a possible marriage date in the future. A very, very long time as I recall. I think you knew I was seeing Colm much more than you were willing to admit, while I was recovering from what I perceived to be your rejection of my hopes. Eventually, I decided to marry Colm. I guess he asked me everyday for over a year. Which is something he professes he wanted to do from the first time he met me. No coward that fellow. Ah, it is such a cross to bear to be so desirable, as well as beautiful, but then not everyone was willing to notice. Like you for instance. I really think you took me so much for granted Danny lad, that you would not look at me so much as look right through me. Usually at some bimbo not in my league.

I don’t want to belabor the differences between you and him, but I found Colm to be most reliable, and willing to commit himself exclusively to me and to his every effort to make me happy. He has never lacked in the "trying to do this" department. He treats me unbelievably well, and committed. Pretty scary words, hey Danny Boy? And on top of everything (the pun is intentional), you, no doubt, are asking yourself right now, is Colm as good a lover as you? The answer is yes, and that is something to be proud of. So don't let it go to your head, neither the one on your shoulders nor the one between your legs, which I guess they didn't shoot off.

While you were good in the lovemaking department, you were lousy in the love sharing department, but Colm is great in both. Someday you may realize that being a bang, bang, banger is not the sum and substance of a relationship, Danny. Even though you thought it could make up for everything else "less important" in your small minded world.

Anyway, Colm is a wonderful guy even though at first he sometimes would be caught up in his working as a physicist continuously coming to grips with the theory of relativity. I guess it just took a while for him to realize that the equation for a solid relationship was more than seeking energy through multiplying mass times the speed of light squared.

If this is too Einstein-ish for you Danny, I'll try to demonstrate. Before I came into his life, my wonderful husband hadn't ventured into oral sex. I was surprised by this since I thought that was one of the prerequisites in college level Sexuality 101, along with learning how to slip on a condom so it wouldn't break. But for some strange reason he didn't do it before me. However, he was a quick study and loved it when I introduced him to that fabulous activity, and showed him how vice can also be so marveous when it's versa. He got the hang of it right quick. And now, wow, he has become world class as he came to understand the old cliché that, once you got passed the idea, you had it licked. And I can assure you he has mastered both - getting past the idea - and giving a licking and go on ticking.

So as good as your over-bloated ego wishes you were, he is better. Maybe not as nervy as you. I recall when we did it in the coatroom of a joint called Fried Eggs and Tootsies Too, or something like that. What a daredevil you were. But Colm is more considerate, and that makes him more understanding and appreciative as a lover.

So, my "wanna be again lover," while I must admit you were talented and I do remember you for the good times (but not the bad), I do not choose to live in the past. And any reminiscing distracts me from the main point of your letter, and the primary question you present, i.e., when do I leave my husband and come running back to you?

Well right now it would be a long trip since you are still in Vietnam and I can't go there. But long or short, what you really want to know is: when will I leave Colm and hurry to your arms and other things? Hmmmmmm, I want you to know that I don't take such an egotistical offer lightly, so let me look in my appointment book and see what would be a good day to do that very thing.

O.K., I've looked, and I've got an open date to do what you wildly suggest. Let's make it April 22nd in the year 2050. If that's good for you, I'll put it down in my little book of things to do later on. In the meanwhile, Danny Boy, don't send any more letters, 'cause with this reply we've got everything set for that big day in 82 years. And, incidentally, don't bother to send a copy of this letter to Colm. He has already seen it, along with your letter to me. We share in this family. Something you never learned.

I thought you should know that Colm laughed when he read your letter and my reply. He said that because of this letter back to you, he wouldn't have to kill you. Such a sweetie.

You would really love him if you ever got to know him, but I guess you won't want to because even though he is sweetheart, he also is the guy you Marines love to quote scripture-wise: "He fears no evil, because he is the - 'meanest muther-fucker' - in the valley."

Oh yes, one more thing, Colm also wondered if your wounds had something to do with serious injury to your frontal lobes. I said I didn't know, but maybe they left enough of your brain cells to allow you to make better judgments in the future.

So that's it, Danny, until April 2050. 'Till then, I'll be thinking about you every time Colm puts his hands and mouth on me, and lovingly touches and kisses me everywhere while I firm things up for him. Such a delight. Thanks for your letter. And good luck in the war if they send you back to kill more of the people you so quaintly refer to as "gooks."

You always were such a poet Danny.

Adieu for 82 - (years that is),

Cynthia

The End

TWIN VENGEANCE

To paraphrase Shakespeare, The sunset this particular day - as seen by a brace of identical twin brothers - portends a saddened rain which will pour downright on their handsome heads.

It is dusk in the High Valley in central California. It is not completely dark as the sun slowly descends behind the Diablo Mountains. Although visibility without lights is limited, one can still see the sloping road winding through a lush agricultural valley surrounded by mountains on three sides. A two-lane bridge that crosses a creek about 50 yards wide is also visible. The creek is almost dry this July, but the bridge is necessary in order to assure no interruption in traffic in either good or bad weather. Traffic is light along the two-lane road.

Two men, dressed in jungle fatigues and wearing dark watch caps and desert combat boots are watching a tractor-trailer truck pulling tandem trailers loaded with beef cattle wind its way down the narrow road. The men are located in an area of brush some 800 feet from the bridge that has been planted with explosives. This deadly ordnance is designed to be triggered electronically from the observers' position. The men spot the lights of the truck and its trailers about a half-mile before the bridge. There are two men in the cab of the truck tractor. The driver is Seamus Stafford, a rancher from the High Valley, the father of twin sons, Jeff and Jim Stafford. The passenger is a migrant farm worker, Mario Herra.

"How did you get this contract?" one of the men concealed in the brush asks."I got a call from a guy who saw my ad in *Mercenary Warrior* magazine," the second man answers. "He asked if I meant what I said in the ad that I would do anything for money. I told him he got that right, and that I had a lot of combat experience in NAM with a strong emphasis on demolitions."

"Who is this guy?"

"I don't know. I didn't ask, and he wouldn't give me any real names anyway. We set up the hit and the price after I checked a few things out to make sure he wasn't a cop. I didn't need any phony name for that. Everything checked. That's why we're here. You cover my back. That's all you have to worry about. I take out the bridge as soon as the truck starts over it.

"Who's in the truck?"

"Don't know. Don't care. You can read about it in the papers tomorrow. I killed a lot of people in NAM and some more since then. I never gave a second thought to what their names were. The bridge is wired. When the truck hits it, I blow whoever is in it to hell and then some. I don't give a damn. This is what I get paid for. Nothing personal. Personal killing is a waste of time and money."

As the two men watch and wait, the truck tractor and trailers make their way down the road towards the bridge. At the same time, a view of another bridge, the San Francisco Bay Bridge, many miles away, revealed that this magnificent bridge was far different from the one the tractor and trailers were approaching in the High Valley.

Brent Worthington, age 55, a wealthy rancher from that very valley, studied the Bay Bridge as it was brightly lighted in all its beauty. He is standing on the balcony of a high-rise apartment penthouse on California and Jones Streets on Nob Hill in San Francisco, just above the financial district. He takes a deep breath as he surveys the panorama that spreads for miles beneath his vantage point, and he extends himself to his full five feet eleven inches in an involuntary gesture as if he were lord over all he sees.

Brent is the brother of Gerard Worthington, age 50. Brent and his brother maintain good physical health and appearance. Neither is slim nor overweight at around 180 pounds, but their physical presentment, nice looking, well groomed, hail fellows well met, belie a deep seeded hatred for and bitter enmity of Seamus Stafford, who is about to meet an untimely demise on a lonely road in the High Valley. The Worthingtons own 70,000 acres of prime cattle ranch in the valley, which holdings are merely part of several sources of income ventures that have made them millionaires many times over. Brent Worthington turns and calls to his mistress, Sherri Lang, whom he maintains in the penthouse. "You're missing a beautiful view love, as the sun sets."

"And you are missing a very naked lady who can give you more pleasure than any old sunset, my darling," Sherri replied lowering herself sensuously on an animal skin rug in front of a fireplace. She lies there with a smile that would melt the strongest of men, especially if they also concentrate on that smile along with her lovely legs invitingly spread for her lover. A picture not likely to be lost on the horny Brent Worthington, whose sexual drive matches his need for power and success.

The fireplace is lighted with natural gas which flames out over brick logs and burns brilliantly without the resulting heat because of a glass shield. "You are right, my pretty vixen. I doubt if even the great master painter himself could refuse an invitation like that." Worthington moves to stand over his mistress and she opens his robe to expose his genitalia. At the moment that Sherri reaches for her lover high up on Nob Hill, her lusty act coincides with Seamus Stafford in the High Valley reaching for the gear shift of the big truck tractor to move the rig and trailers into lower gear in order to safely negotiate the narrow bridge he is approaching.

As Seamus reaches the bridge and moves his powerful load unto it, Brent Worthington and Sherri are engaged in the ultimate sexual union in the penthouse in San Francisco. Close to climax, Sherri cries out, "Oh Brent, darling! Oh darling! I'm there!"

"Oh yes! Oh yes! I'm ready too. I'm ready to explode," he grunts forcefully at the same instant that the Stafford tractor and trailers are halfway across the bridge and are met with a devastating explosion. A horrible resulting fireball disintegrates the full rig, its two human occupants, and all of the cargo of cattle.

*****

Two years later the murder of their father still had not been solved, although Jim and Jeff Stafford believe, and keep insisting to any authority who will listen, that had to be orchestrated by the Worthington brothers. Unfortunately, they haven't been able to prove it. The local Sheriff, a political hack and obsequious pawn of the Worthingtons, wouldn't be competent to solve a case of shoplifting caught on video, much less solve the assassination of Seamus Stafford. The FBI entered the case on the basis of interference with interstate commerce, but the trail was cold and the Feds concluded nothing other than it was a highly professional execution perpetrated by a person or persons unknown who covered his or their tracks well. The file remained open, but was no longer actively worked. Thus the FBI hadn't done any better with its investigation than the hapless Sheriff, in spite of passionate claims by the Stafford twins that the Worthingtons must be behind it all.

"It's all a bunch a crap, Jeff," Jim announced to his twin brother who bore a close physical appearance. Jeff was the younger, born 23 minutes after Jim. Each brother, now age 24, stood 6 feet 1 inch tall, with comfortably erect posture, and weighed about the same at 200 pounds. They reflect similar muscular development from bodybuilding and athletics over many years.

"Time to exact a bit of personal justice," Jim said almost matter-of-factly. "I am going to kill the Worthingtons," he vowed. His tone was filled with undisguised disgust and hate over the criminal justice system as he voiced his draconian pronouncement, which was more than an idle threat.

"Yeah, right," Jeff replied. "What are you, nuts? Violence to rectify violence. A great wrong to correct a greater wrong. Really makes no sense," Jeff countered, looking strangely at his anguished brother.

“You got that right, brother. The first wrong was evil. The greater, so-called second wrong, will be justice. And in this case two wrongs make a right. Anything else I need to explain to extricate you from your wimpy outlook?” Jim fired back.

“How much alike you and I are,” Jeff said sadly. “Not just our brown hair and blue eyes, but the way we present ourselves in the same way; sort of like Dad did, confident but not arrogant. So how can we be so different in this instance? Tell me that Jim, if you can.”

The answer to Jeff's question, ignored by Jim, lay in the difference between these identical twins who physically were almost mirror images, but whose personalities developed independently and sharply distinct. They enjoy the same intelligence level, well above average I.Q., but Jim is strong willed like their father was and usually stubborn in his mind set. Whereas Jeff is more flexible in his attitudes and responses. They are comfortable financially, but not exceptionally wealthy, except for the land holdings they inherited when their father was murdered. Their mother, a beautiful woman, died of cancer when the twins were 12 years old. Added to this was the violent death of their father. Jeff worked at adapting to these painful losses in their young lives, but Jim never came to terms with either of these terrible events.

By comparison to the Stafford twins, Brent Worthington, who has gray hair, and Gerard Worthington, with dark brown and gray hair giving him a salt and pepper effect, are not as handsome as the twins, but they are better than average looking and carry themselves well, full of confidence ingrained by more than their wealth. Their father, grandfather, and great grandfather were ranchers and agricultural leaders in the High Valley so their self-assurance evolved from a generational wellspring. Presenting a formidable demeanor consistent with life as hands on ranchers since they were children, they reflect the luxury that hard earned, exceptional wealth provides.

Each is worth many millions, and they enjoy true upper class status. Feared in the valley, most of High Valley citizens pay lip service to the brothers' obvious special status, even though these good citizens in their private thoughts view the Worthingtons as unworthy rich, ruthless bastards, who have too much moneyed power.

The Worthington brothers, Ivy League educated, use their academic background to advantage along with turning the substantial wealth into greater wealth through sharp and selfish business dealings. Much of which involved crushing smaller ranchers and farmers through mortgage controls and product channeling as the singular most powerful distribution source in the valley. Thus the brothers' community stature is nurtured by fear and an irrational awe of financial giants similar to certain family dynasties in the Eastern United States who enjoy prestige and respectability in spite of totally immoral business and political dealings for generations.

The Worthingtons are married. Brent has two children, a son and a daughter. He also has his mistress, Sherri, in San Francisco, whom he visits several times a month. Gerard is faithfully married. Not because he was disinterested in sex outside of marriage, but rather because his personal mistress is power; the kind of power that substantial wealth provides. He has no children because he is infertile, which adds to his lust for power and control. The moral, or more accurately, amoral standards of the brothers Worthington are on a par. Their embrace of situational ethics is unfailingly predicated on a convenient morality of the moment. An epidemic rampant in the world of business these days, for which the law is sadly impotent in developing a cure.

Motivated by reasons of their bent morals, in spite of their religious facade at church, they are close in their heated denials of any suggestion of unscrupulous conduct, and such challenges are not allowed to get in the way of their constant goals of acquiring more power and more wealth. Both are extroverts. But only superficially since they are comparable in their suspicious analysis of every person they meet. This is especially true of those with whom they must do business, either through dominance or finesse.

Bright and dangerous as enemies, the older sibling, Brent, is particularly dangerous when opposed, and not as superficially diplomatic as Gerard in his business dealings. But both are deceivers at heart, and allow nothing to frustrate their ambitions or plans, even when resort to murder may be required. They attempt to disguise their malevolence and lack of true regard for others with well-practiced displays of personality. As a result they control party politics in the valley with the same iron hand in which they attempt to control the valley's economics. An accurate account of these dangerous men must also include their public personae, nothing more than disarming facades; always smiling, always glad handing, but always equally ready to cut off one's genitals when necessary. Their untimely, violent demise at the hands of Jim Stafford would undoubtedly be praised by their many financial victims as untimely only in that it was long overdue.

Jim's plan for their removal from the planet focuses on the Worthingtons' hobbies, which include sailing, ownership and running of thoroughbred horses, and their passion for flying a beautifully restored World War I vintage airplane they own, a Sopwith Camel. The Camel is a thing of beauty conjuring up delightful images of World War I aviation.

By contrast to the Worthingtons, the Stafford twins' father, the late Seamus Stafford, was a hard working rancher, strong willed and self-made. Seamus had learned ranching and agriculture from his father, as well as inheriting discipline through a long, family line of ranchers and farmers. He had no education beyond high school, but he believed the twins should go to college.

Jim, however, wasn't enthusiastic about college, principally because he hated to be away from the land he loved so dearly. But their father insisted and he was not a man to be denied. Jeff, on the other hand, was excited about college, and being a well-rounded athlete, he was able to attend the University of California at Berkeley on an athletic scholarship. Jim, also a better than average athlete, made the Cal football and baseball teams, but only as a walk on. They both did well in football and baseball, but Jeff excelled in football and made several All American teams in his junior and senior years.

Upon graduation, it was Jim's fondest dream to return to the High Valley and spend his life with his father in operating the ranch and farm. Jeff, instead, decided to try his hand at professional football with the San Francisco Forty-Niners when drafted in the NFL second round. He was pleased to be with the Forty-Niners since this would keep his athletic base reasonable close to the ranch. But he had no desire to immediately return to the High Valley and assume a rancher's life.

The twins have many friends in the valley, and are well respected. But they are also regarded carefully by those who were not their friends, particularly because of their quick to anger when provoked. Jim was the most feared. A loose cannon when defied and not one to back off from confrontation. Jeff is slower to anger, but equally formidable when pushed to the wall.

Socially both Jim and Jeff are sexually oriented in a normal context, and they genuinely enjoy women. This allows them to experience a fairly satisfactory sex life with the local girls, as well as some interesting liaisons with generous college women at Cal. Their sexual mores are not distracted by, nor in conflict with any moral qualms about sex outside of marriage. Without such unnecessary baggage they are comfortable with an instinctive understanding of what is right and wrong. This does not arise in any particular ethical sense, but rather because they are genuine young men who live by a rule of reason unencumbered by complicated religious controlling agendas. Their simple rule is: If relationships are consensual and don't deliberately hurt anyone, why accept the nonsense that they are morally wrong?

Their ambitions, on the other hand, are bifurcated. Jeff wants to succeed in professional sports and when he has done that, then and only then, does he plan to return to the land. Conversely, Jim's great passion is the land, and every day he was away from the High Valley nagged at him. He is a part of the land. It is deeply ingrained in his character. He spends hours riding along the green and brown hills dotted with grazing cattle, savoring the way the river runs through the hills and ravines, and watching with wonder as the land turns fiery red at sunset and a mist of tulle fog enfolds the last rays of the dying light in a tender embrace. His love affair with the land was the single constant in his life since his father's tragic death.

Because the Stafford ranch and the High Valley are Jim's very essence, what he manifested in response to their father's murder was distinct from Jeff, even if not entirely different. Jeff was not given to shooting from the hip, but Jim lived with a savage storehouse of emotions that smoldered relentlessly since their father's violent murder. He became obsessed with revenge, which he viewed as a crusade for justice. Especially since a personal vigilante justice appeared to be the only kind that would bring the Worthingtons to account for their egregious and murderous misconduct.

Jim regularly reminded Jeff that he would never get over their father's death. He reiterated his passion so much so that he was able to unqualifiedly reject any suggestion of immorality in seeking retribution against the Worthington brothers, whom he was convinced orchestrated the murder. “We can't wait for the law to do the work," Jim admonished Jeff after he demurred on Jim's suggestion of self-help. “It never will.”

"If I could do anything to expedite the criminal justice process, I would," Jeff assured his brother. "But I can't, and I am painfully aware that hate is a two edged sword. It can kill you as much as the object of your hate. I only wish I could disabuse you of the notion of vigilante action," Jeff explained as calmly as he could in the face of his brother's searing anger. "I want no part of any plot to kill in order to affect justice, especially killing the Worthingtons. You sound like the guy being questioned for jury duty who said, ‘I'm as impartial as the next man, so let's get on with it and bring the guilty bastard in so we can give him a fair trial and then hang his ass.’"

"When did you become a candy-ass, Jeff?" Jim retorted sarcastically.

"The day you decided to be the sole judge, jury and executioner without bothering with the niceties of due process. I don't want anything to do with any of your plans, nor do I want to know about any stupid decision you are contemplating to lower yourself to the Worthingtons' level."

Jim did not respond to Jeff's admonishment about vigilante action. As they were talking, they were standing on an upper deck of the main ranch house, which overlooked a broad portion of the lush six thousand acres of agricultural and cattle grazing land spread across a low lying plain that sloped gently upward towards the east creating an abundant watershed that naturally irrigated the farming and grazing portions of the ranch. After a long pause during which Jim feasted on the panorama of the land that ironically filled his revenge seeking soul with calming pleasure, he turned to Jeff and with a look that seemed almost demonic and said, "I will do it with or without you then. It needs to be done, and there's nothing left to argue about."

Two days later, intensified by his hate and knowing no easy solution to his quest for justice, Jim drove up to San Francisco to see if he could find anyone hanging around the sleazy joints in the tenderloin area who might be able to advise him on how to take out the Worthington's without implicating him, other than creating some natural suspicion, but with no hard proof. Posing as a graduate student from the University of California doing research on crime and punishment, he frequented several of the garbage pits in the tenderloin, but until the seventh place he stopped, he was not able to obtain a lead as to anyone who could provide a sophisticated plot for murder. After buying a few drinks for a couple of unwashed specimens sitting at the bar, he got an indirect referral to a unnamed person who, from time to time, ran an ad in the *Mercenary Warrior* magazine.

Following up on the suggestion, Jim went to a second hand bookstore on Geary Street that was piled high with used books and back issues of many magazines of eclectic tastes. Among these he found the ad placed by an unidentified person who, unknown to Jim, was ironically the same one who had blown up their father. Reply was to a box number only, to an individual who claimed to be willing to do anything for the right price. The referring scuzzballs in the bar remembered a guy who held himself out to be a super expert with high explosives, and Jim thought it would be fitting if his invoking of justice against the Worthingtons included their violent demise by explosion as he believed they had directed against his father.

He then rented a P.O. Box under an assumed name and sent an inquiry to the other box listed in the ad that was a few months old. He got a quick reply two days later advising him to call a certain number (turned out to be a pay phone) at a specific time on a specific date. Jim followed through with the call, which then led to a face to face meeting with a rather hard looking individual at the Wharf. No identities were exchanged, but after discussing his interest in an explosive device, the contact said he would get back to Jim in a few days, presumably to check out Jim's status as something other than a police informant. On their next meeting the contact advised Jim that for a reasonable sum he could furnish him with an explosive device that would let him to clear tree stumps and any other bothersome items he needed to remove.

Jim chuckled at the phraseology, explaining that he was a bit more interested in something sophisticated along the lines of an altitude bomb which would not be primed and triggered until a certain altitude was reached, and would allow, for example, an airplane to take off and reach a definite height before the explosive device would arm and explode.

"O.K., then I will get your something to clear out very tall trees," the mercenary replied with a grin. "But it will cost you a great deal more. If interested, I sure can make it available tomorrow and will provide you with detailed instruction on its installation and altimeter triggering setting." The deal was struck and the contact, never identified by name, made the sophisticated weapon available to Jim twenty-four hours later, for which Jim paid twenty-five thousand dollars with no questions asked.

Jim then returned to the High Valley and proceeded with his plan to install the altitude bomb in the reconfigured, dual cockpit, Sopwith Camel, vintage 1918. This prized possession of the Worthington brothers would be flown, weather permitting, on Sunday mornings for an hour or so, either together or individually, if at least one of them was not out of town. Jim smiled as he noted that the Worthingtons' passion for flying the classic airplane, which the brothers never allowed anyone else to operate, was about to become the perfect vehicle for their deaths. Armed with the deadly device, Jim implemented his plan by carefully staking out the Worthingtons' hangar where the Sopwith Camel was stored when not in actual use. The routine of the Worthingtons made this phase of the vengeful plan easiest to formulate and carry out. He wondered why he had waited so long to bring justice to that pair of asshole scoundrels, as he thought of them with deep down hate.

He noted with amazement that security was primitive considering the value of the classic aircraft, and was provided only by locks on the hangar door and a quality lock on the only window which was located on the back side of the hangar, out of view of the roadway. These rudimentary security devices were augmented by a burglar alarm, which surprisingly was electrically controlled by wires running from a nearby power pole. Cutting the power was so simple a task, that the device was virtually worthless as an alarm system.

He further concluded that if in the unlikely event the device was a silent alarm system (since a noisemaker type would be of no worth at the small airfield which was used exclusively by the Worthingtons), he could still break into the hanger and install the bomb in two minutes flat. Thus, he would be long gone before any physical response to the silent alarm was likely to be taken since the private facility was some fifteen miles from the closest Sheriff's substation.

Prying open the hangar window in order to circumvent the locking device was easier than expected, and Jim was able to gain access and plant the bomb, which was not large, under the forward seat in the airplane. He set the trigger mechanism to detonate at 3000 feet, an altitude certain to be reached by the Worthingtons the next time they flew, hopefully together, since the High Valley was already 1000 feet above sea level. "But even one of these bastards at a time is better than nothing, Jim said allowed as he planted the fatal device. After completing his macabre business that took only a few minutes, Jim exited by the window he had entered and secured it with some putty tacked at the corners to make it appear that it had not been opened. He then returned home undetected.

It was a grim business that he was about, but he admitted to himself that he hadn't a single qualm and that he felt better than he had at any time since that tragic night his father was blown to bits. All appeared to be going well, except for one problem that arose as the plan waited for final implementation. The following Sunday after Jim planted the bomb, the Worthington brothers had a glorious outing in their Sopwith Camel, poking holes in the sky for almost two hours well above the 3000 foot triggering altitude. Then they landed and put their beautiful toy away, totally unaware that they had been sitting on a weapon designed to assure their instant removal from the planet. As a result of still being very much alive, they went back to business as usual, plotting whatever scheme they could pursue to tighten their stranglehold on the valley.

Jim had been watching the hangar through binoculars from a hilltop some distance from the airfield. He couldn't believe the Worthingtons were able to escape death and return safely to continue their corrupt existence. "Goddamn it all to fucking hell," he swore loudly, "now I have to break into the fucking hangar again and remove the fucking bomb to see what the fuck is needed to make it function properly."

That very night he broke in again since he was fully determined to correct any problem with the bomb and replant it within a day or so to be ready for the next flight of the hated Worthingtons. I'll get the damn thing out of there and make it work right, he thought as he climbed in the hangar window and approached the plane to carefully retrieve the deadly device from under the forward seat. But at the moment he succeeded in extracting the weapon from under the seat, the lethal charge exploded in his hands. Jim and the Camel were reduced to bloody fragments. Vengeance, seemingly perfectly planned, imploded on the revenger.

*****

As he buried his brother next to their father and mother in the cemetery of the church they had attended as a family, Jeff tried to make sense out of the Jim's violent death. An investigation ensued over the next few months focusing on what Jim was doing in the Worthington's hangar, but Jeff never said a word about his brother's hate filled mission. And no criminal action was ever taken against anyone, including the Worthingtons. The lingering and now virtually dead investigation into the murder of Seamus Stafford was filed away as unsolvable.

At Jim's funeral Jeff wept as his twin was lowered into the earth of the High Valley he loved so dearly and at such great cost. Then he reflected sadly that, except for maybe Jesus of Nazareth, whose death was divinely predetermined as the ultimate salvific act, circa 33 A.D., every person's death is untimely. One either dies too early or too late. Adolf Hitler, for example: way too late. A year old toddler killed by a lunatic nanny: way too early. Jeff's dear brother's death at only thirty years on earth was woefully premature.

Later, as part of the probate proceedings following Jim's death, Jeff sold the ranch to a corporate agricultural conglomerate to keep it out of the hands of the Worthingtons. In doing so, fate took another strange turn. Unknown to Jeff, the vicious Worthingtons were the majority stockholders of the conglomerate to whom he sold the ranch and stock. Irony built upon irony as this fateful twist solidified the Worthingtons' iron hold on the Valley.

When the sale closed, Jeff moved permanently to San Francisco. He seldom goes back to High Valley. Mostly only to visit his parents' and Jim's graves. He never stays long. The memories are too painful.

In contemplative moods Jeff often sadly recalls the poetry of Sara Teasdale and her poignant observation:

It was a spring that never came,
But we lived enough to know
What we never had, remains;
It is the things we have that go.

The End

ERNESTLY SPEAKING

The man arose with a hangover. One of several thousand in his life, but he got used to them long ago. He belched as he scratched his growing belly and remembered that he and his friend, Ava, at last recall, had been drinking from a goatskin. It might have been good wine, but at that point he couldn't tell. Nor did he care. But he did care about his husky-voiced, Ava, his for the moment at least; a sloe-eyed beauty, blessed with a magnetic, tigress-like enchantment, whose breasts were - not like white elephants of which the man was so fond - but rather like white forbidden fruit in the Garden of Eden of which the man was wildly enamored.

With bloodshot eyes he quietly looked out at the ocean from his Bimini retreat, and wondered if he would live long enough to be an old man irrevocably intertwined with the sea. He then noted that the sun had also risen, but not with a hangover as he did. Instead it flared from many hundreds of hydrogen bombs exploding every second, which made the man's head hurt more at the thought. "Maybe I should take a ride this morning across the river and into the trees to clear my head before I awaken Ava," he said softly as he embraced the sea he knew and loved so well.

"God, she's beautiful," he continued softly and wistfully, "even after a night of reckless abandon. I dread the day I will have to say farewell to her arms. But then, I have come to accept the inevitable, although it will be like facing a brace of killers.

"Ava dearest you are so magnificently beautiful. I will never forget the first time we made love when we were on safari in the green hills of Africa waiting for the torrents of spring to subside as we sought to understand what the leopard was doing in the snow near the crest of Kilimanjaro. So much like our own lives with all their mystery.

"I can see why Frank never got over you, much less Mickey and Artie. Once the bell tolls for me on our delicious relationship, I don't know where I will find another moveable feast as magnificent as you. I just might become a man among men without women.

It's winner take all, or winner take nothing in this game of love, which all too often ends with death in the afternoon. Sort of like running with the bulls, something they never do up in Michigan where I once visited but never returned.

"Not likely there will ever be another island in the stream of my life like you, my extraordinary lady full of sensuous grace. And then there will be no more to have. Only to have not. But until that dangerous summer when you leave me, which I must accept in our time, I will try not to crumble like a fifth column built on quicksand.

"I must write a letter from Cuba one of these days to my old friend Scotty F. I will write in my old newsman mode. I think that would be best. I must tell him of the short life of a guy I once knew, Francis Macomber, who put a shotgun in his mouth along a lonely and big, two-hearted river, rather than in a clean well lighted place. Macomber was too kind to make a mess for others. Even though his heart was broken by the loss of a quintessentially sexual woman, very much like you, Ava. Who like a cat in the rain, always seeks shelter as its instincts direct.

"I'll miss you, my beautiful Ava, when you too flee. But no sad songs right now. I think it's time to feast again and pretend that my life has always been true at first light and is something more than just another piece in the art of fiction.

"For the moment I will love before the movable feast moves on, and then, when it's time, I too - like Macomber - will go out with a bang."

The End

THE DAY SAMMY HEAD DIED *

---

* Colonel Donald Eugene Holben, USMC, provided the introductory pages of this story, along with the basic concept before his death in January 1999. His family graciously allowed me to complete the story my great friend envisioned. Michael Patrick Murray.

Sammy Head, formerly, Corporal Samuel H. T. Head, United States Marine Corps, heard the loud thunk as the trap door under his feet dropped into the retainers. What he did not hear was the perceptible cracking that indicated his neck had broken cleanly without severing the head. This brought a smile to the face of his executioner, and one other person on the platform, General Hazel E. Rathman, USMC. Interestingly, the gloved hand of the official executioner was nowhere near the lever that released the trap door under Sammy's feet.

The hand was definitely feminine. But no one noticed this except the official executioner. The events leading up to this unusual event in Marine Corps history, found Sammy Head wrapped in an upper body straight jacket with his hands strapped behind his back and firmly secured to a chain around his waist. His legs were bound with leg irons attached to a chain carefully calculated to permit him to climb the 13 steps up to the gallows platform. The fatally sentenced corporal, at his request, wore no cover. His shaven head radiated dead white from a lack of sunshine.

The rest of Sammy's complexion was ruddy, however, reflecting his German-American heritage. The condemned Marine had been called front and center of the Marine Detachment serving at the Army Prison at Fort Leavenworth, Kansas, for his last formation. He faced the detachment Sergeant Major and listened with customary Marine-like attention as the Sergeant Major published the following order:

THE WHITEHOUSE

Samuel H. T. Head:

Your request for Presidential Clemency has been thoroughly reviewed by this office. It is my opinion that your desertion in the face of the enemy was most reprehensible, leading in part to the ultimate defeat of your unit. Which proud unit suffered 100%

casualties and caused it to cease as an effective military entity. This conduct on the part of a Marine, particularly a noncommissioned officer, cannot be tolerated or condoned.

Therefore, it is my considered judgment that the sentence in your case is more than appropriate and will be carried out at the earliest opportunity. The following administrative details may impress upon those present, if not yourself, the revulsion I feel toward a Marine who would desert his fellow Marines in battle, thereby causing irreparable harm and many deaths as a result. It is hereby ORDERED that you suffer:

(1) Death by hanging.

(2) Immediate interment with noose intact, i.e., with no mortuary services.

(3) Burial will be in the cheapest wooden casket with no internal upholstery. The executioner's special graveyard will be your final resting place.

(4) A copy of your dishonorable discharge, and this order, will be secured on your chest on the outer garment worn by you upon burial.

Helen R. Corfam

President of the United States

*****

President Corfam was not the author of the condemnatory notice of denial of executive clemency in Corporal Head's case. That was accomplished by General Hazel E. Rathman, USMC, for the President's signature. General Rathman's anger, which had motivated the denial of clemency, was quite understandable. Actually, President Corfam would have granted clemency, but that decision would probably have resulted in serious, adverse political consequences for her, and she wasn't the kind of politician who took unnecessary political risks.

As Sammy Head's body was dumped into the ugly, cheap wooden casket, after he was declared dead by a physician present at the hanging, it was arranged on its back, noose intact, as ordered, with the death notice pinned to his chest garment. Afterwards when most of the witnesses had left the scene, except for General Hazel E. Rathman, a strange event occurred.

The executioner noticed that General Rathman checked every detail of the President's order for compliance. Then as the executioner turned his back to direct his truck driver to back up a little closer, thinking there was no use in carrying the cowardly son of a bitch any farther than necessary, out of the corner of his eye he saw, quite distinctly, General Rathman bend over the dead Marine and spit in his face.

"Strange lot, these Marines," he said to himself, "as many soldiers as I have officiated at their final dance, I have never seen anything like this. I wonder what would bring a man to such an ultimate disgrace?

*****

This is Sammy Head's story. Sammy wanted to be a Marine more than anything else in the world. And he tried to be a good one. The Marine Corps did not fail Sammy. It's just that, in the end, he simply didn't fit. If only he and the Corps could have met on some common ground, he could have been, and would have been one of the finest among the finest. Here's what happened.

Sammy was convinced that he was born to be a Marine. His father had served proudly on active duty in the Corps for twenty-five years. He had been outstanding and he retired as a Sergeant Major. Seemingly out of shame, he sadly refused to attend his son's final appearance on earth, but to the end Sammy loved him and was very proud of his daddy. The late Corporal Head's great grandfather, who he never knew, had been a non-commissioned officer in Marine Corps during the Civil War. He had participated a few years before that awful war in the raid at Harper's Ferry and the capture of John Brown, the infamous radical abolitionist. Sammy's grandfather, on his father's side, had been a Marine in World War II and Korea.

The military, and in particular the Marine Corps, was in Sammy's blood. He knew it and so did everyone associated with him. He was a Marine junior, and proud of it. Army and Air Force children are referred to as "brats." But Marine and Navy children are known as "Marine or Navy Juniors."

When Sergeant Major Head, then himself a brand new Corporal, USMC, determined that it was time to start young Sammy's military training, he made a wooden replica of the older M-16 service rifle, which was being replaced by the new service rifle, the US Rifle M-124. This was a unique military rifle weighing only 4 pounds when loaded with the maximum magazine load of five rounds. Every military man involved in its development (95% plastic, 17-caliber sabot round, laser sight) wanted at least a 30 round magazine. They didn't get what they wanted.

President Helen Corfam, the first American female to hold that powerful office, succeeded to that status from Vice President following the death of her predecessor. The late, former president had died in a drowning accident early in his first term while frolicking in the White House pool during a drunken party with Hollywood celebrities. He had quite a plethora of precedent for such high jinks from the previous administrations of JFK, LBJ, and WJC.

Helen Corfam was not in office long before she had decided that firepower of a 30 round magazine for the new M-124 rifle in the hands of the infantry was not needed because she erroneously perceived the world as a place of peace and tranquility, which she was convinced existed among all peoples. She made this egregious mistake despite the advice of a few of her military advisors who were not sycophants, of which there were damned few, and she lost her perspective in the myth that such position helped her image and bolstered her leadership role of peace through demonstration. Of course, President Corfam, like Bill Clinton, had never served in any military service and being a liberal of the first magnitude, she actively hated anything that involved the military. But she wisely refrained from saying so in public.

When introduced to the M-124 rifle, she factiously referred to it as that "cute little gun" which she understood had been made on a bull pup plastic stock. And she was delighted that the rifle could be hung from one's belt, rather than carried "John Wayne style" with swaggering machismo. Actually the regular carrying method of the M-124 was slung across the chest since it was too small to do any type of manual of arms. The M-16, the rifle it replaced, was bad enough for that purpose, and always looked sloppy at best.

The deciding feature of the M-124, as compared to an M-16 rifle, as far as the new president was concerned, was its compatibility for use by men and women. The light stock gave it this redeeming feature. Unfortunately, on the down side, the sabot round it fired was only effective out to 150 yards and the laser sight was only good for about 25 yards in bright sunlight. It was forced on the infantry types, who finally had to give in to pressure from the Air Force, and feminist organizations that represented women's' right to "volunteer" for, but unlike men, could not be required to fill combat billets.

Combat veterans, who composed much of the ranks of the Corps, were of the unqualified opinion that women should not serve on the line in combat. This was for several good reasons that only experience could provide, but added to these was the glaring disparity between women being able to volunteer for combat roles, but also able to decline any order to fill a combat billet as a woman might choose. Men enjoyed no such luxury, and if there were ever to be equality among the genders in the military, this clearly was a distinction that made a great difference.

Sergeant Major Head's homemade training rifle for Sammy, resembling the old M-16, was made of hardwood. It was a beautifully grained piece of ash that he had finished with a clear polyethylene finish. It did not look like a real rifle. It was too pretty. That made no difference to the Federal agents who came to get the Sergeant Major's real guns. They took Sammy's wooden training rifle as well, even though they could see it wasn't real. This left Sammy to train only with a broomstick. Sammy's father had realized early on that President Corfam's agenda vis-à-vis guns, which included the totally unconstitutional Fire Arms Confiscation Act she had maneuvered through Congress, a process she initiated from her first day as president, would force the declaration and forfeiture of the collection of fine firearms handed down through his family for generations. He had taken the precaution of sending these beautiful antiques, plus his favorite target pistols, hunting rifles, and shotguns, to a friend in Canada where there were strict gun laws but nothing quite as absurd and silly as the ones that existed in the United States that had been proposed by President Corfam's predecessor before he died as a lousy, drowned drunk. The late, ex-President, had been an unqualified high tech pitchman who had been elected on the Reform Party ticket.

However, at the risk of a sure felony conviction with a mandatory 25-year sentence for mere possession of a handgun, Sammy's father had kept his favorite target pistol, a .45-caliber semiautomatic for protection of himself and his family. It was well hidden from the Federal Gun Confiscation Bureau agents of the gun control agency created by the new confiscation law, who tore his quarters apart knowing that he was a gun owner. They had learned this by a review of the honest declaration and registration of privately owned firearms he was required to execute in order to live on a military base; which the agents immediately examined and then moved against. So much for being honest, but as a parting insult the senior confiscation agent swore - perjured is more accurate - that he "accidentally" shot Sammy's dog while carelessly unloading his weapon prior to entering his vehicle. He didn't even apologize, of course.

The agents then went on to the next set of quarters and brought out the few private weapons the occupant, a First Sergeant, owned. They laid them out in the driveway and drove over them with their van before collecting them up and tossing them in a heap in the vehicle. The First Sergeant was brought out of his quarters at gunpoint, hand cuffed, and in leg irons. His military career of 27 years had come to an end, as he was facing at least 100 years in prison. A gleeful remark was made by a baby-faced, twenty-two year old, confiscation agent who never gave a thought to joining the military.

"These dumb jerks are easy pickings. They register their guns, like all good Marines are required to do, and all we have to do is come aboard and pick them up. Just bring along lots of cuffs and leg irons. Now that the stupid son of a bitch of a Sergeant Major has all these guns registered, he has to have them some place. We'll be back. Maybe at midnight.

"And we'll catch that SOB and send him to the slammer forever."

The next time they came, they brought a backhoe and dug up his yard, front and back, but found nothing except Sammy's broomstick. The outrageous conduct of the gun confiscation agents, instead of discouraging Sammy, actually encouraged him to become a member of the Marine Corps, the one government institution that he firmly believed still functioned on an honorable level. So Sammy remained devoted to his precious Corps, and he enlisted immediately upon graduation from high school.

His father and mother were proud witnesses at his enlistment ceremony, and they wished him well as they sent him off to boot camp at Camp LeJeune. Marine Corps Recruit Depot, Parris Island, South Carolina, which had been the starting point of hundreds of thousands of Marines over the years, had been closed on the order of President Corfam because she thought it was redundant for training purposes, as she wrongly concluded that Camp LeJeune was big enough to handle East coast Marine Corps boot training, as well as its other missions.

Sammy was excited. He was finally going to become a bona fide Marine just like his daddy, his granddaddy, and his great granddaddy. And, maybe someday, he too would become a Sergeant Major. His grandfather, who had served proudly in the Corps in two big wars, used to regale him with fine stories about the old China Marines when he served with Derby Ross, who in the 1950s, was the senior Sergeant Major in the Corps. Stories about the Springfield '03 rifle, and all the men he served with in WWII and Korea, were part of Sammy's education.

Sammy's father had served two tours in Vietnam, but his stories were never as good as granddad's. A lot of those Nam stories were about how bad the M-16 rifle was and how many of his buddies either used the AK-47s they captured, or died trying to get the accursed M-16 to function. The problem was never fixed. The last investigating team from HQMC sent to Nam to resolve the problem arrived in 1970. But they never did solve it, and the last Marines in force left Vietnam in 1971 with the same lousy rifle. There really was only one thing good to say for it. The Air Force liked the M-16 because it fit their women security forces needs better than the heavier M-14. Obviously, infantry considerations were secondary even then. Grunts just weren't politically correct enough.

So Sammy did everything that was required of him to become a good Marine. He trained with distinction, making Private First Class upon graduation from boot camp, and then Lance Corporal only five months later. Less than six months after that, he was promoted meritoriously to Corporal and was proud to become a noncommissioned officer in the Corps by the time he was 19 years old.

Then his world stood on its end on June 25th, sixty years to the day that the North Korean People's Army, (the NKPA), had invaded South Korea in a war that began in 1950, which war Harry Truman ridiculously called a “police action.” Old Harry, the would be atomic saint, would never be confused with a rocket scientist. The NKPA had launched its invasion in June 1950, without warning by crossing the 38th parallel demarcation line that divided North and South Korea as a result of the consistent stupidity of Harry Truman and Secretary of State, Dean Rusk, caving into Joe Stalin towards the end of World War II. The same devastating advance 60 years later, once again without any warning, took place on another fateful June 25th. This was no "police action," 60 years later any more than the 1950 Korean War was.

The weapons these many years later were more sophisticated, of course, except for the dinky, lousy, "cute little gun," that had no sustained fire power or killing power, and which presented logistic problems of major magnitude. It was virtually worthless for up close and personal combat. But American troops had to carry it due to President Corfam's ill conceived idea that the "peoples of the world" were truly peace loving. Helen Corfam, obviously, wasn't any smarter than Harry Truman. Even these many years later, however, the tactics were pretty much the same, starting with horrendous artillery barrages running the width of the peninsula, and then terrifying advances by tanks and infantry following air strikes over a period of sixteen hours. Lulled by the shortsightedness of the United States Commander in Chief, the South Korean Army had learned to accept the loss of support of tens of thousands of U.S. Army troops foolishly withdrawn from the Korean sector, leaving only a couple thousand assigned to the ROK Army. And the result was as bad as the June 1950 attack by the North Korean People's Army (the NKPA). On that earlier terrible day in 1950, the well equipped and well prepared NKPA invading force was only confronted by ill trained, ill prepared, under supplied, and very soft, peacetime U.S. troops stationed in Japan who were rushed to Korea to try and block the immediate devastation of people, civilian and military, that the sorely inadequate 1950 South Korean (ROK) defense plan could not prevent.

Also, as they had done in 1950, the North Koreans, now sixty years later, filled the ranks of retreating civilian refugees with armed military soldiers dressed in civilian clothes. This enabled the infiltrators to decimate weaker pockets of the ROK's defenses at every opportunity. As a result, allied aviation sent into action against the invaders made no distinction about who was civilian and who was military.

Which was easy to justify when flying high above the fray, and many civilians were killed or wounded by cannon, missiles, and bombs which were allegedly intended only for the defeat of the enemy. Such massive destruction of civilian noncombatants found precedent in World War II and the Vietnam war, especially in the latter under the code name, Arc Light. These were B-52 bombing missions (one B-52 could carry 54,000 pounds of bombs). Bombing during these missions was usually conducted from 35,000 feet or higher by radar that could penetrate even the most dense cloud cover. The people on the ground did not even know bombs were falling until they hit. The North Vietnamese called the arc light raids, “whispering death." And a million Vietnamese civilians were killed by such raids and artillery fire. As in 1950, Marines in this new war 60 years later were once again hurried to Korea. This time from the 3rd Marine Division stationed in Okinawa. Thus the response time was much less than in 1950 when the lst Marine Provisional Brigade had to take up the perimeter defense of Pusan after the NKPA had nearly overrun the whole peninsula and South Korea was being crushed.

Corporal Sammy Head, USMC, was part of the 3rd Marine Division, rushed into action in the new war, and he found himself in the thick of the fighting against the North Koreans within days of the full alert for assistance to the Republic of Korea forces. What may have been acceptable for aviators, however, became a nightmare for the grunts, as hordes of civilians were pressing south not much ahead of the bulk of the advancing NKPA. These multitudes were fully integrated with NKPA troops in their midst, or who were prodding them from behind, threatening them with certain death if they did not keep pushing on deeper into South Korea. As a result, thousands of civilians came under what is euphemistically referred to as "friendly fire." In his advanced infantry training at Camp Lejeune following boot camp, Sammy was advised that sometimes civilian casualties were a necessary adjunct to engaging the enemy. This was especially true with aviation because it was hard, if not impossible, to distinguish the good guys from the bad guys when zooming in at 600 knots loaded with incredible weapons of destruction. He also was taught that often ground troops were faced with a similar problem when calling for artillery support, or even when facing a mix of civilians and enemy troops up close and personal.

"Sorry to say, but some civilians simply get in the way," the instructor, a combat vet casually noted, "and you will have to shoot at them without necessarily wanting to." Such matter of fact observation was not callous. It simply was the reality of war.

Sammy thought this was rather strange because he remembered learning in history class in high school that obedience to orders to kill civilians was not a defense in the trial of German and Japanese war criminals following World War II, and in Nam where an Army lieutenant was court-martialed for killing some hundred or more defenseless civilians in a Vietnamese village. So how was he to reconcile obedience to orders issued to him as a Marine when those orders caught civilians in fire supposedly directed at the enemy. He didn't know the answer, and he wasn't allowed to ask the question. So it remained unsettled in the back of his mind.

What made matters worse was that Sammy just did not know, and wasn't taught, that the basic defense of obedience to superior orders, outlawed generally after World War II, was still a valid defense if a soldier carried out an illegal order while mistaken as to a fact relevant to the order and the law involved. This was too sophisticated a concept of law for Sammy. That was exactly the situation that Sammy encountered in South Korea, however, when 60 years after the start of the first Korean War, it came to pass that the horror of massacres inflicted on refugees in other villages early in the 1950 Korean War, were revisited in Sammy's war at Yongdungpo, near Seoul.

This was where Corporal Sammy Head found himself being required to kill people, seemingly indiscriminately, as if selection were even possible much less likely. He was a trusted squad leader, and his squad was given orders to stop the advance of anyone, without exception, military or civilian, who would attempt to cross a vital bridge over the Han River, which bridge was to be blown up, when and if, necessary. The bridge would be vital to the enemy's advance. Sammy did as he was ordered, and he became a witness to the random death flowing from his hands and those of his squad imposed on men, women and children reaching out as they were forced at gun point to surge forward across the bridge by NKPA infiltrators hiding among them or at their backs. Sammy, being a good Marine, followed orders he often did not fully understand as to their underlying reasons, and he blew away dozens of people, young and old. But it didn't take long for him to begin brooding about the many young children, some only babies, who he personally had dispatched from the planet. All of which was done pursuant to military orders that probably flowed all the way from the top in the name of the current, militarily dumbest Commander in Chief who ever occupied the Office of The President except for the draft dodger called “Slick Willie”.

Sammy didn’t like what he was ordered to do and before too long he became seriously disheartened. After two days and nights where too much shooting into the crowd had to be done, that was abated only by intermittent breaks for sleep in two hour intervals when the refugees fled back from the bridge, Sammy, violently sick at heart by the seemingly unrelenting massacre of the innocent, could no longer contain himself. Notwithstanding his desire to be a well-disciplined Marine, he discovered in spite of all his family background and all of his fine Marine Corps training, that he was compelled by psychological reasons to leave his position with the squad and approach his platoon commander. The officer was a young second lieutenant with no previous combat experience. He tried to explain to the lieutenant, almost tearfully, that he couldn't go on killing people any longer, and he asked to be relieved as squad leader and be allowed some respite from the gruesome horror of participating in what he considered unnecessary and unjustified killing. Sammy could not overcome his revulsion at an alleged requirement to kill innocent people.

He was wrong, of course. The highly distasteful task of killing some civilians in order to take out infiltrating military forces to save American lives in the long run was necessary, and it was a lawful order he was obliged to follow. An analogy could be drawn between the order given to Sammy and the dropping of atomic bombs on principally civilian populations in Hiroshima and Nagasaki in World War II. And it was on this common ground that the Marine Corps and Sammy, who wanted to be a good Marine, were unable to meet.

His request was refused, of course, with a resounding response, "Get your ass back to your squad, Corporal, and do your job. What kind of crap is this?" With that, Sammy was ordered to move his squad to a closer position along the critical Han River Bridge while the combat engineers would be setting demolitions to be ready to blow the bridge if it became apparent that continued defense of it would be impossible. Sammy reluctantly did as ordered, but he was well trained to obey orders, and he returned to his squad. He then radioed back to his platoon commander that the two remaining squads of the platoon would be needed soon to cover the opposite flank of the bridge because people were once again crowding at the far end, some four hundred yards away, and appeared determined to proceed forward. The lieutenant responded by placing the full platoon, all forty-one men, in position along the bridge. But when the refugees at the far end saw what was happening and sensed that the bridge would be destroyed, they surged forward in an attempt to cross before it was blown. They really had nowhere else to go. The North Korean infiltrators would shoot them is they tried to turn back; so going forward seemed the most logical route of escape. But Sammy's platoon was ordered to open fire and the Marines cut down the masses moving towards them from the far side as soon as they started across.

This didn't stop those who were not hit earlier by the Marines' rapid fire or by the NKPA infiltrators from the rear of the crowd.

And the carnage mounted. The dead and wounded piled up, and the terrified mob climbing over them, longing for safety, soon proved to be unbearable for Corporal Sammy Head. He could no longer accept his part in the savage butchery of human beings. As if in a terrible nightmare, he stood up and cried out, "Enough! Enough of this slaughter! I can't do this anymore!" The other members of his squad looked at him and wondered what the hell he was doing as Sammy threw down his rifle and ran up to the platoon leader and shouted that he couldn't be a part of anymore killing, and that he was leaving.

His comrades upon seeing the confusion and the strange behavior of a United States Marine who had been taught the ultimate in discipline and teamwork, closed in on Sammy and the platoon leader. In doing so, they became dangerously bunched up at the moment two North Korean jets flew out of the hills and dropped napalm on both sides of the bridge. The clustered platoon was caught in the inferno that killed hundreds of the civilians and many of the Marines. Each and every one of the rest of the Marines who were not killed, was severely injured by the napalm.

A reinforcing company from a battalion of the 3rd Marine Division moved up to assist Sammy's company, and recovered the dead and wounded Marines while the engineers carried out their original plan to blow the bridge. When Sammy was released from the Naval Hospital in Okinawa, to which he had been evacuated after extensive surgery in a field hospital unit, he was immediately confined to the brig at Funtema. The charges implying the disgrace of cowardice, included leaving his post and desertion in the face of the enemy, which criminal misconduct caused the death or wounding of 100 % of his unit.

He was tried by general court-martial three months later, and sentenced to death along with a dishonorable discharge. No one else who had killed men, women and children from the air, or on the ground, at or near the village of Yongdungpo and the bridge over the Han River was prosecuted for anything. It didn't matter who killed whom. Civilians were simply incidental casualties of war once again. But cowardice and desertion in the face of the enemy, an enemy who ironically had caused all the killing to happen, was unforgivable in the eyes of the command. Sammy Head had stuck his neck out once too often, no matter how compassionately motivated he had been. The last time he stuck his neck out, it had a rope around it.

The surviving refugees at the bridge near Yongdungpo, who were able to move, rushed past after the napalm fires had diminished and before the bridge was blown. Many were killed by other Marines for their efforts. Sammy Head also died for his efforts. But it was at the end of the executioner's rope because he had rebelled against killing so many innocent refugees - who had been infiltrated by NKPA soldiers - which soldiers were bent on killing American and South Korean troops and civilians. This was a Hobson's choice Sammy couldn't cope with. If he had continued to indiscriminately kill, he probably would have been awarded a medal, maybe more than one. Instead, he got a face full of saliva from a Marine general whose son was in Sammy's platoon and who was killed at the Han River Bridge.

General Hazel E. Rathman's son was burned to death by the napalm. At his burial ceremony at Arlington National Cemetery, he was awarded, posthumously, the Bronze Star with combat "V", and the Purple Heart. General Rathman was heartbroken, but proud of her son at the same time. Who could blame her for hating Corporal Sammy H.T. Head, U.S. Marine Corps?

Sammy didn't understand any of this on the day he died, strangled and with a broken neck at the end of an executioner's rope. He wanted to be a Marine, but he didn't want to kill people he was certain were not his enemy. And he didn't want to believe that part of the reason he was given a gun and sent to war was to kill people, other than allegedly bad people who were called the enemy. When push came to shove at that terrible bridge, Sammy couldn't accept that some innocent bystanders might also be caught in the crossfire, and he had to kill them too. He couldn't appreciate that his personal, moral misgivings had to give way to doing what was necessary in war. And all of the killing he was asked to do, even of civilians who were caught in the middle, was just part and parcel of the horrible business of war. Terrible decisions of life and death, innocent or guilty, have to be made every day in war. This was no different.

Harry Truman may have had a problem condemning 250,000 civilians to atomic death, but he made his horrible decision to drop not one but two atomic bombs (one alone would have been enough) on innocent Japanese civilians, because he thought it was morally necessary so an estimated one million other lives would be saved. Talk about anguished situational ethics. Some people challenge the number of lives saved as conveniently inflated, and refer to this a statistical justification. In any event if old Harry could make tough decisions, why should Sammy be allowed to disobey orders that were designed paradoxically to save lives by killing hundreds of innocent human beings? A real Catch-22.

The laws of war, especially as delineated by the Judgment at Nuremberg handed down in the trial of the Major German War Criminals following Word War II, leave the military person with nothing more than a confusing choice in such matters. Obedience to an illegal order of a superior is not a defense to carrying out the illegal order. But disobedience of a lawful order issued by a superior, no matter how odious or morally reprehensible to the soldier the carrying out the so-called lawful order might be, is a crime.

On the end of that bridge in Korea on that fateful day there was no way that Sammy was able to reconcile this moral dilemma, or even begin to understand that he had a duty to carry out what he perceived as something terribly immoral. What he also failed to understand is that some orders are as hard to give in combat as they are to be carried out. And in Sammy's life the perception of having to kill people, who didn't deserve to be killed, suddenly became reality. But sad as this was, the killing was necessary and lawful under the laws of war. He just never got a handle on it. Sammy was not experienced enough to fully understand that if the Commandant of the Marine Corps said, "Sammy saddle up, we are marching into hell today," the only question Sammy should ever ask was, "What time do we launch, General? And not to ask if this was a good idea.

No matter how much she hated him, General Rathman should not have spit in Sammy's face as he lay ready for burial without honors because he had failed to carry out lawful orders to kill innocent people.

This is not the Marine Corps way. But she was a mother, and her son died as a result of Sammy's inability to meet with the Marine Corps on a common ground on the bloody, dehumanizing fields of combat.

Sammy was too far removed from any of this after his death sentence had been affirmed and carried out following the exhaustion of all appeals over a period of almost three years on death row. Thus he was spared the humiliation leveled upon him by General Rathman's cruel response to her anger and pain.

No medals were awarded to Sammy Head, a fine young man who wanted to be a good Marine, but came up short. Instead, he simply lay in the executioner's field, decaying without embalming, with dried spittle on his face and a dishonorable discharge pinned to his breast.

The End

WHO KILLED DICK

Dick was a private eye. A real sleaze bag. Somebody offed him. He deserved it. But the law - sometimes a one-word oxymoron in Los Angeles - requires that whoever killed Dick, who in truth deserved killing, must be prosecuted. And if convicted, the killer had to be killed for killing. Strange world out there even in L.A. If it isn't the weirdest town for application of the law, how does one explain the acquittal of O. J. Simpson?

As for Dick, well a not so bright broad name Monique "the mouth" Lewdly had worked her way up in political circles because she was willing to start at the bottom. The mouthy Monique had slipped over to Dick's digs to hire him to do a private snoop job for her. When she got to his pad, however, Dick had taken leave of his skanky world with three souvenir .38-caliber slugs in his ugly head.

Monique was scared witless - a short trip at best - and was about to exit the scene of Dick's dastardly demise, when she heard a voice coming from the room next to the one Dick was lying in.

Monique whirled to face the faceless voice, and immediately recognized the owner of that familiar tongue. It was Tad the Cad, a mendacious politician, which really is a redundancy. The kind who wouldn't know the truth if it hit him in the mouth.

"You sacred the hell out of me," Monique cried. "What are you doing here in Dick's den? Did you blow Dick the prick away?"

"Don't be cute, Monique, you trash heap. You are a more likely candidate for blowing things than I ever would be. I came here to get Dick to do some work for me. But I got here after the fact of his well-deserved departure from the planet. Hollywood and otherwise."

"Yeah, sure," Monique replied sarcastically. "This could be more of your down and dirty response to all of the bad mouthing you've been getting, or should I say not getting, now that none of your political buddies will send you any interns after Slick Willie gets through with them. What irony, especially after all you did to stand up for them."

"Up yours, you mouthy bitch. It went down just like I said. I came here to pay mucho dinero to get Dick to dig the dirt about a certain someone named Linda who seems to like giving people a bad trip in the press and on T.V. I was hoping he could make a case, real or manufactured, against this so-called friend of yours, as I recall, who has been taking folks down to a level they are not accustomed to, unless of course, it was of their own choosing."

"Yeah, O.K.," Monique snickered, ignoring the friendly jibe. "But so what? Even if Dick wasn't cooling by the time you say you arrived, how did you expect him to pull anyone's loins out of the clutches of the bad trip lassie?"

"I didn't really care," Tad answered. "I only wanted him to stick it to the broad who has been putting it to some folks I admire, such as me, over something that was nobody's business except mine, and the sweet young things who always looked up to me just like they did with Slick Willie.

“Old Slick was doing all right until Linda dressed up his life with the stain of scandal. And I understand he was going to divorce his plain Jane wife (a major understatement), and marry some bimbo like you and live happily ever after, once he came off his homely - airy hill - of marital misfortune."

"Stick your sarcasm where the sun doesn't shine, bad Tad. I know Slick Willie very well, and I'd bend over backwards just to hold his cigars. So can the sarcasm. I only wish I had a flat head so he put his beer stein on it while I am helping him to blow away his troubles. If you didn't do the deed to Dick the dick, who do you think did?" Monique asked as she helped herself to a piece of fruit from Dick's counter top. Which was strange because Monique usually didn't talk with her mouth full.

"Don't know and don't care," Tad replied after watching with genuine fascination the way Monique finished off the banana. "All I know is when I was arriving, I saw a car going hell for leather. Hey, that sounds kinky. Going down Coldwater Canyon Road I mean, and it looked like Morris the Cat was driving. It could have been him, especially because he got caught with his tail hanging way out after Dick exposed his kitty box which was filled with $200.00 an hour litter."

"Hey, you may have something there," Monique chimed in. "It's a start, and it doesn't matter if it was fat cat Morris who offed Dick or not. We can leak a rumor to the media and they will take it as gospel, of course, and run a banner headline right next to the rest of the - everybody knows who done it but nobody's doing anything about it - stories. You know the ones - where guys like O.J. are looking all over hell for the real killer - except in the mirror. And add to that, Jesse

Jackass, who denies screwing with the IRS. I understand he's a friend of that new white guy, Michael Jackson.

"You figure a bold, bullshit rumor will do it. Well that sounds good, Monique. I don't give a rat's rear about who snuffed whom in this case. I only want one thing, and that is to discredit the porky blabber who has been dishing the dirt about affairs involving my privates, whoops ... I mean privacy. None of which could be considered sexual relations according to Slick Willie's dictionary. Even if is - is - is. And now that Dick has crossed over the river Styx, I need someone else to dig up enough muck on the broad and get her off my back. Then I can get back to helping several sweet things kneel down in reverend adoration in the chapel. You know the one. It's called, Saint Oral's."

"Hell, I can do it for you," Monique replied quickly. "All I need from you are a few statistics about the precise depth of your relationship with your fellow parishioners. Or is fellow a misnomer? Whatever! Once I get the score, I will transpose it into something other than ugly rumor. Something really nice to say about you, if that's possible, which I'll contend I got straight from the tootsie who talks too much after she taps into the friendship of people she allegedly treasures. And I'll make her out to be a big liar about the bad stuff. Is it a deal?"

"Deal," Tad agreed, while looking longingly again at Monique's mouth with frank amazement and lusty appreciation as she devoured another “Chick – eat – a — Banana.”

The End

DEVIL MAY CARE

We are drinking fine cold beer at an hour past midnight as a night cap to top off a delightful evening.

Shortly before this we had dropped off our dates after a fun outing including dinner, dancing, and a little grab ass. But not the penetrating sex kind. Especially not with those very cautious ladies. A couple of beers to relax was a natural thing for two university upperclassmen after a lovely evening with a brace of college women we were getting more interested in than we had considered likely in the beginning of our relationships. It was intended to be only fun and games since each of the participants was convinced that we all were too young to be thinking about serious commitment to in-depth romances. And yet my roommate and I continued dating our coed friends exclusively for several months. So much for just fun and games. Maybe it was cupid who was playing games as we reprised the evening and enjoyed the beer in our room in the Delta Kappa fraternity house located along fraternity row at the University of Illinois.

In our house, like most of the others, the members factiously and stupidly referred to the fraternity as “I Felt a Thigh,” a pun which had been bouncing around for at least a hundred years, and which, because of political correctness, had been resurrected to replace a different tasteless joke, that used to be considered funny in the old days, that made reference to the frat's name as: “Rape a Dame a Day.” The latter phrase by this time in our so-called civilized world, even though no real offense was intended, was particularly objectionable to feminists.

As was our custom at least once a week after a night of socializing, my roommate, Adam Cavington, a fine Episcopalian young man majoring in philosophy and psychology, and I, Patrick Brendon O'Casey, an Irish Catholic (what else could I be?), majoring in philosophy and history, decided to engage in one of our many philosophical discussions and excursions through which we resolved some, but not quite all, of the many problems of humanity; none of which, in our youthful arrogance, we considered to be insurmountable.

"I realize this was your umpteenth date with Judy," Adam noted. "About as many as I have had with Cindy. I actually lost count a couple of months ago. And I think the four of us are either getting quite used to each other, or too lazy to move on to other pastures.

“Either way, however, I don't see much progress on your part in the let's hit the kip department between you and the great looking Judy. I call her Jugs Judy, but only with you, because you understand why," he joked inoffensively. "My god, what a great rack."

“And your point is?" I retorted. "Hell I doubt if you've even been able to cop a feel with Cindy, these days. What's her stage name? Miss Frigidaire?"

"Hey, can I help it if my date of late is a card carrying Baptist? These things take time. Maybe I should concentrate on Mormon girls. I understand they know how to have a really good time without drinking and smoking. And one out of three ain't bad."

“Yeah maybe you should, or maybe your should just keep working on Miss I’ll Never Uncross My Legs Until Marriage, and you will finally score about the time of the second coming. Which in your case, would be your first with lovely Cindy. Lot's of luck."

"I just have two words for you, old buddy, and the second is you. The first one begins with the universal "F" that you already know."

I laughed and then observed, "Hey, this is really good beer. Where'd you find it?"

"Got it at Tony's beer depot. The guy said it was a fairly new name called Sam Adams, and noted it was getting big on the market. Used to be a well kept secret for a few years, but now it's better known and for good reason, it's really terrific. Came back on the market a while ago after a hundred years or so of ceasing original production by some relation of the celebrated John Adams. Tony said I was sure to like it. So I thanked him for the suggestion, and I reminded him that anyone who doesn't like beer is certain to be missing the second best thing in life. He asked me what the first thing was, and I assured him it could be anything he wanted it to be, just so beer was never less than second."

"I'll roger that," I chuckled. "So what pressing philosophical question shall we ruminate on tonight in our weekly ritual of solving all of the pitfalls of the human condition? Other than, are we getting closer to getting into the knickers of our lady friends now that we have had many dates and have sort of boiled things down to an unexpected, exclusive interest in them. In that regard, I might add, I am happy to report that I was delighted to see how Judy was really warming up tonight. But I suspect the old saw about mortal sins of the flesh kept getting in the way. If you think Baptist girls are tough to crack, you ought to try Roman Catholics. Jeez what an obstacle the phobia about mortal sin and eternal damnation is, as it haunts people to become emotional cripples," I said with a sarcastic laugh.

"Hey, that sounds like an opener for tonight's discussion," Adam replied, "something about mortal sin from both philosophical as well as theological perspectives, but not too heavy on the latter please. Even though this will take us on a slight detour around the more important issue of when do we get down to some serious lovemaking with Judy and Cindy."

"O.K.," I said, "this looks good as a consideration of a mixed bag of philosophical and theological conundrums. But I must note up front that I won't go easy on the theological, even though you deserters from the true religion, Roman Catholicism, as opposed to your Episcopal or Anglican Catholic, may have a hard time keeping up. I warn you about this because I want us to address the concept of hell; that real or imagined, fact, fiction, myth or legend, that flows from the construction of a deified archetype which was called the Force in Star Wars, and we more enlightened folks traditionally recognize as God or the Godhead. Admittedly, this will result in more theology than philosophy, but it should be stimulating to plunge into the issues both in the abstract as well as metaphysically."

"Wow, that's quite a plateful you propose," Adam said shaking his head, "especially for you Roman Catholic bead mumblers who are so steeped in tradition that change and new ideas create terror in your hearts. Why don't we just discuss the nature of being in a narrower sense, and then worry about hell if it applies. Such as, do we exist because we know? Or do we know because we exist? And more importantly, do we know that we know? That is, how do we really know anything apart from our own perceptions as to whether or not we exist, and if we do, whether or not we can actually know anything at all."

"Save the neo-sophistication crap for your philosophy professors," I chastised. "They might pretend to understand what you are asking, even without actually understanding. That's what makes them professors, I guess. But for our purposes, let's keep it basic. We know we exist. And we know we think. All I ask is: Have you ever thought about the ultimate of questions that deal with what really happens at the end of our time on this mortal planet? And is there an afterlife? In this framework I have a question that has been on my mind a lot lately. It goes like this: Assuming you have a child, what could your child possibly do that would prompt you to send him or her to a place of eternal punishment? And I mean literally eternal, as in forever and ever. Like without any end whatsoever."

After I threw this out for Adam's consideration, I gave him a little time to weigh the challenge, and then I continued. "Let's pursue this in the context of myth vis-à-vis reality relating to the concept of hell in the context of Dante's Inferno, complete with fire and brimstone, and unceasing suffering. Of course, Dante presented his perspective on hell and damnation primarily for his own vengeful satisfaction as a political treatise on how his enemies should end up, but then he added a bit of window dressing to make hell appear to be a more universal punishment for alleged misconduct, such as lovemaking between actually innocent young lovers. And thus his word painting of the terror of a place called hell, with all its several levels of increasing suffering depending on the extent of the so-called mortal sins that supposedly caused the inhabitants to be there, was truly frightening in its horrible and terrifyingly descriptive totality."

I then added, "As far as I am able to logically deduce, and this is purely my personal perspective so take it in that sense, I don't know if there could be anything that bad. I suppose some people would say that they could send a child of theirs to everlasting, never ending punishment for something they did that would be as egregious as the conduct of a Hitler, or Stalin, or Mao Tse-tung (Mao Zedung). I don't know. Of course, all this presumes that there is such a place of eternal punishment as hell. Which suggests that hell probably is not a place or condition here on earth since it could not be eternal if it is on earth since the earth will go out of existence in about five billion years when the sun dies. This hell, a place or state of being then, is something we must assume for argument sake is beyond earthly confines, notwithstanding that some people might suggest we experience such condition or place right here on earth during our lifetime in order to purge ourselves of bad karma created by our transgressions, or sins, if you prefer to call them that."

"Yeah, all right," Adam reclamored. "Let's stipulate that such a place or condition, or state of being, actually exists outside of our present status on earth. The question as you present it, if I understand your analysis correctly, remains simply: Is there really anything that would cause you to disavow your children, who I'm sure you would profess to love unconditionally, and send them to a place of never ceasing punishment?"

"That's it in a nutshell, I replied. "And to me the answer is that there isn't anything my child could do that would bring me to impose such an eternal, draconian condition on him or her, even if he or she killed their mother and all of their siblings before my eyes? And if I could not do this, imperfect as I am, no matter how terrible that conduct, then how would a perfect being like God, our eternal Father filled with perfect, unconditional love, send someone to hell and condemn him to brutal punishment and damnation forever? It would be a contradiction to profess unconditional love and then send someone to hell, no matter how terrible one's conduct. This would place a limitation on God's perfect and unconditional love, and His perfect mercy too, and thus make Him imperfect."

"Tell me," Adam said a little uncomfortably, "how did we descend into this much theological muck and mire? I enjoy the philosophical, but who really knows anything about these theological mysteries? It's all speculation. Even the very existence of a place or condition called hell. So who cares?"

"Well, obviously the devil may care, if he exists, and a lot of other folks too, but for different reasons," I responded rather gravely. "People have been scaring themselves to death, or being scared to death by preachers, ad nauseam, who daily rattle the sabers of eternal damnation, hell fire, gnashing of teeth, and all the other terrifying, religious clap trap. So millions of people, maybe billions who believe there really is a hell, care about this shit as you poetically imply by calling it theological muck and mire.

"They care because they are afraid not to. And they also want to believe in hell as a place for bad people to get their comeuppance for their terrible conduct. This gives the good people, who are afraid to be bad, some semblance of consolation against all the awful stuff people do, or have done, to them.

“Note that I emphasize that they are good people who behave, but only because most of them are afraid not to. Except, maybe for those substantially evolved ones who genuinely behave because it is the right thing to do in and of itself. The mix is sort of a potpourri of goodness, fear, and consolation all wrapped up into one."

"Hey, isn't that great," Adam responded sarcastically. "Maybe we will go to hell, however, because we are unwilling to forgive the sinner rather than enjoying his certain condemnation for his sins, while at the same time we further console ourselves with an arrogance that assures us that God's justice requires that sinners will go to hell, but we won't do that with conviction mainly because we are afraid to be sinners too, and are afraid to be even mentioned in the same class with the truly bad dudes. What a paradox. And that's only one of many that confront not only us Christians, but any member of a religious faith that believes in the concept of hell."

"O.K.," I said. "So much for theory. But getting back to my question. If we, who are not perfect, can not - and I emphasize can not - send our children to hell no matter how screwed up they got because we claim to love them unconditionally, then how could God, whose unconditional love is perfect, do so? How could a perfectly merciful, loving God send anyone to an everlasting hell, if there is such a place?

"I'm not trying to box you in on this," I continued. "But maybe I can do an end run around tricky phrasing and suggest that God really doesn't send anyone to hell, contrary to the demagogues who pretend they speak for the Almighty when they threaten us with sailing down the river Styx and dropping over the falls of fire into an eternal abyss.

What I clearly mean is, I don't believe God actually sends anyone to hell, whatever and wherever that is. Assuming that such a place or condition really exists.

"But, rather, He created this so-called hell as a place for those who choose to be somewhere else, other than with Him. You know, like the fallen angels and other dummies who had the chance to know God and be with God. But for whatever reasons: pride, money, power, and other stuff, they choose to reject beatific vision and eternal presence, as a matter of their own free will. At the same time some who did know God, later rejected being with God, like the great angel Lucifer did by choosing not to stay with Him in a place or state of being called heaven or paradise. Hard to believe old Beelzebub would be so fucking stupid, but that's the biblical spin."

"All right," Adam retorted, "you have now taken a free will end run around the question of hell, and you've made it easy for God to wash his hands of the responsibility of sending anyone to hell by suggesting that people go there because they choose to as of matter of exercising free will, but not otherwise."

"Yeah well, I think you got my point," I answered. "So what's your take on this?"

"Well," Adam replied, "I don't know why they intelligently would make such an awesome choice, but if that's the case, then it shouldn't matter what dumb, terrible, stupid, or awful things any of us do in life, just so long as we don't commit the one unpardonable sin, as the bible suggests, which is to choose not to be with God and to turn our backs on the spirit, the Holy Spirit of God if you will, who we used to call the Holy Ghost. Thus, according to your theory, we can be as bad as we wish, and yet never go to hell unless we deliberately, while looking God in the face, say we don't want to be with Him, and instead as a deliberate act of our free will choose to go where those souls who make such a foolish choice would go. Hard to believe anyone would be so fucking dumb, but then there's always the unbelievable assholes with no moral understanding. Child pornographers come to mind."

"All right," I noted, "technically it can be reduced to that basic form, but maybe it's not that cut and dried. Because if we don't practice goodness while here on earth, then it may be most unlikely that we will choose to be with the ultimate of all good, i.e., God, at the end of our lives because we chose all the rest of the time not to stand with the good. But, at the same time my point is that no one under my theory is ever sent to hell. And you can only get there if you deliberately choose to be there. Isn't that what the unconditional gift of salvation is all about? Provided one freely wishes to accept that marvelous gift.

"As Martin Luther taught, and the Roman Catholic Church finally agreed after taking a long time to see the light, all the good works of a lifetime do not create salvation or guarantee it. This is because salvation is a pure gift of perfect love from God through the Son we call Jesus the Christ, and that gift is unconditional and complete. So, in essence, I can't save myself. Because I am already saved. All I have to do is to accept that complete gift of salvation and not reject it, and then I'm sure to be with God, no matter how much I have deliberately or negligently goofed in my lifetime."

"Sounds too easy," Adam answered after a bit of refection. "What the hell, Patrick, as a Roman Catholic you must have spent your entire life so far worrying about backing into Heaven by somehow getting absolution for all your mortal sin fuckups before you die. Otherwise, all those so-called mortal sins, like screwing pretty girls you weren't married to, would be a cinch to get your ass delivered nonstop to Hades the moment you left the planet."

"Yep," I concurred, "and now you have the essence of our personal control over our destiny. The essence of free will vis-à-vis theological controls. The latter controls are imposed to persuade us that if the preachers and other wanna be God appointees didn't scare the bejesus out of us by the threat of going straight to hell if we don't act in a certain way before we draw our last breath, our whole life style could get potentially beyond the control of the controllers. Thus the threat of hell in this way becomes the most powerful of controls and motivators. What better vehicle for obtaining and maintaining a death grip over our free will."

"Hey, what are you some kind of iconoclastic nut?" Adam asked with a grin.

"No," I replied emphatically. "Just an observer of the human condition. You ever watch the lunatic T.V. evangelists on Sunday, or any other day for that matter? And I don't mean just those pitchmen and women who wear enough makeup to cover a whole troop of Ringling Brother performers, and enough gaudy bangles that would pale the crown jewels.

“I mean those clowns who pitch fear, and more fear, and then even more fear, of eternal damnation if you don't conform to their version of the rules of the road on the highway to heaven. Rules that include sending them lots of money to maintain their ministries, while adorning themselves with Guggi shoes and three thousand buck suits and dresses. It is laughable because through their intimidations we actually allow ourselves to become afraid that we could be shunted off to eternal fire. But it is really nothing but an excursion into the ridiculous that finds so many people actually taken in by scare tactics who are led into conforming according to these goofy preachers' blue print for salvation. It is so amazing how many suckers send these clowns millions of dollars to keep their terrorizing message flowing behind the patent facades of puffy, blow dried hair, and eyelashes longer than a German shepherd's tongue as they perform in their theaters of the absurd."

The phone rang just as I was about to challenge Adam further with some questions that might prove more difficult than trying to solve an esoteric math problem of major proportion like the Pythagorean theorem.

"Hi," I said without knowing who was calling. "Hi, yourself, Patrick," the caller said back. "It's Judy. I knew I wouldn't be waking you or Adam even at this late, or should I say, early hour. What major world pressing problems were the young philosophers solving now instead of thinking about the wonderful time we had earlier this evening?"

"Ah, let me see. I think we were talking about what a poor Irish lad like myself could do to convince a nice girl like you that she doesn't have to be inflexibly nice, all the time," I replied with a chuckle.

"Oh, you mean like the times you seem to have more arms than an octopus, and I can't move fast enough to avoid your not very accidental grabs."

"Yeah, something like that, Judy darlin'."

"I was just teasing, Patrick. Actually I guess I was preaching to the choir with that glib comeback. Because I know that while you may be a bad boy, there never has been a suggestion that you are a few fries short of a happy meal. And I know you are brilliant enough to see through my so-called resistance to your lusty advances." Judy paused for a moment to gather her courage and then said, "Plus I am confident that you must know how I feel about you, and how I share your desires with equal interest," she said calmly, although a bit surprised by this spontaneous confession of her sexual feelings.

"You can count on it being mutual," I chimed in, "especially if you are the happy meal."

"See what I mean," Judy said laughing. "You are incorrigible, but maybe that's why I like you so much, and that's really why I am calling, along with thanking you for a very nice time last evening. But not to digress from my precise purpose, I want to remind you that … Well, O.K., … I'm Catholic, and that means I'm not supposed to enjoy your touchy-feely games. But to be honest I have actually only been pretending, and I thought I'd confess this on the phone rather than face to face since this is somewhat embarrassing for me."

"Hey, no reason to be embarrassed. I pushed you a tad hard and I apologize. Subtlety is not my long suit. But I didn't know you were pretending when you resisted. I thought it was just part of you being a Catholic girl," I answered hoping to sound genuine.

"I appreciate your kindness, Pat, but I should be completely candid about this, and about us. I really like you, and I do enjoy your sexual overtures, even if I have to play the vestal virgin game. I never mentioned anything about that status and how I might fit into the equation, but I thought you ought to know by this time in our relationship, and okay I'll confess I still am. Nothing to be afraid of, nor disappointed about, so I'm not complaining.

"Hey, I never said anything about your status. And quite frankly it isn't any of my business. Neither one of us was expected to have lived in a vacuum before we met. So I ask no questions, and I didn't care what may have been in your past," I said hoping to assure Judy as best I could about the vestal virgin rap. "But I hasten to add that I never thought of you as a stereotypical Cosmo Girl either, who believed the baloney of how sexual experiences were possible without a moment of consideration for love and emotional feelings. The so-called sexual revolution has brought us more than a litany of sexually transmitted diseases, but even worse, it has extracted an exorbitant price on our emotions, especially for women who find nothing comforting about a bim bam, thank you ma'am approach where foreplay consists of rushing to unlock the door so the players for the night can tear their clothes off.

"I think you a darn fine woman, Judy, and a first class lady, so don't let your reluctance to acknowledge a shared desire and interest translate into something negative. I want you to understand that while it's undoubtedly true I want you physically, that isn't the alpha and omega of my feelings. I want you in every way, and this may sound old fashioned and corny, but it's the truth. I want you because I love you in every way, along with a natural physical desire. So there I've said it at last. I love you, and I respect you, as well as wanting you body and soul."

"Well, thank you, Pat. That's quite a personal homily, and I'll admit I share your feelings in return. I'll also add that some of my reluctance with you was because I had a bad experience some time ago, and I don't want another one. It was with someone I thought I cared about a whole lot, and the feelings were supposed to be vice versa. But the vice was all versa in the end. And now the main thing I wish to be up front with you about is not my past, but the present, and to tell you that, in spite of some previous disappointment, I do feel the same as you do, and I am genuinely interested in you physically, as well as in all the other things I truly like and admire about you. So I think I can quit pretending, and instead suggest that perhaps we can work out some sort of compromise about my feelings for you, physically and otherwise, and resolve any fear of my plunging into perdition if I give vent to those feelings."

"Funny you should say that," I came back, "because Adam and I were just philosophizing about that very sort of thing. Hell fire and damnation, et al. But I've worked it out in-depth. So if you'd like, I'll explain it all in just two points."

"You always could reduce issues to their simplest dimensions, my love, so let's hear this two point solution to my moral qualms."

"O.K, for openers, sex outside of marriage, assuming that both participants are single and at least old enough to make adult-like decisions of this sort, and I am talking about heterosexual sex, may have some moral taint attached to it, but it is not a great moral transgression. Nothing more, at the very best, than venial sin, and probably not even that. Whatever so-called venial sins amount to these days. Maybe something less than the whoppers Slick Willie Clinton committed with his scandalous, abusive, lying conduct towards Monica, Gennifer, and Paula; just to name a few. He was totally immoral.

"But there is nothing mortally sinful about you and me making love. So when, and I suppose I should say, if and when, I finally persuade you to let me actually make love to you completely, you may feel comfortable in the knowledge that what sexual pleasures we will enjoy are far from being hell damning mortal sins. Remember you are only accountable for what you truly believe as to what's right and what's wrong, so there's no use attaching a mortal sin basis to consensual sex between adults, especially when they truly care about each other. At best, maybe it's a venial sin. But so what? Like, who is it hurting? And in the final analysis I think we make up for these little sins, venial sins that is, as we progress through life and catch a lot of flak from the rest of the world. But there's nothing mortally damning about loving someone, especially when the someone is you, and you are the someone I hope will love me in return. There simply can be no hell fire and damnation in that scenario."

"Well if that's all there is to it, then what's the second of the two points you alluded to?" Judy quipped. "Seems like it may just be frosting on the cake."

"All right, the second is that hell is a highly overrated, fear concept, imposed by those who would control us body and mind. And, even assuming arguendo, that there could possibly be such a place as hell, eternal hell to boot, it is only for those who by the sheer exercise of their free will choose to go there and to stay there until they change their mind. Now I believe that you personally would never choose to go to hell and reject being with God, so there is nothing we can do in the lovemaking department, even if our lovemaking was some kind of carnal disobedience, that could or would ever relegate you to hell. And that's the sum and substance of why we should now plan on our next date for a delicious repast of loving that we both have wanted for a long time, and, until now, I have not had to courage to speak openly about. In short, it ain't wrong to begin with, and even if it were, it would only be a minor wrong. There is nothing to fret about. It has nothing to do with your choosing to go to hell simply because you will enjoy the wonders of our loving each other."

"Wow, what a performance, Patrick lad," Judy said with a chuckle. "I'm overwhelmed. I can see why - as you have told me a few times - that you set a record for getting kicked out of religion classes in your Jesuit prep school. You spent more time in detention, or jug as you Jebbie preppies called it, memorizing Shakespeare than you did in class. And now you appear to be a master at seduction, but in a sophisticated way. You sure you believe all this, or are you just a young man so horny, you'd say anything to get me in bed?"

"I'm all of those things and more," Pat replied. "But I am genuinely serious about this, and it isn't just to get you in the sack, although the idea is very moving. I do care about you, and I do want to make love to you."

"You sure about this, or is this just part of your master's program in seduction?" Judy asked laughing.

"Hey dear lady, it's genuine, and I hasten to add what we are about is not a sin, and we aren't going to hell when we do make love. What time should I pick you up tonight?"

"You seem pretty certain I will concur in all this," Judy said with good humor.

"Why not, you know we will be lovers sooner or later, and sooner seems a lot better than later. I promise the following: one, I will be gentle, and, two I will find us a nice accommodation, like the Hotel No Tell, and not the back seat of my car."

"You are scaring the hell out me, Patrick, but arousing my curiosity at the same time. So scared or not, I will really think about this, and will let you know when you pick me up at seven tonight as to whether or not it is a full blown go."

"Hey I like your phraseology, but I won't dwell on the pun. See you at seven, and for want of a better joke, for a whole lot of heaven."

"O.K. But, Oh God, that was corny. Your performance has got to be better than your exit line. See you then. Ta, ta."

"What the hell was that all about?" Adam asked as I hung up. "I've been trying to piece together the snippets of conversation I could only catch on hearing your end of the conversation."

"It's about Judy and I closing the loop my friend, and I'll let you know in the morning if the closure was complete. No details, of course, because a gentleman never kisses and tells. But I'll let you know if it was a thumbs up or down. And that's all I am going to say about the lovely Judy and me at this moment.

"So now let's close another loop while I can think about something else besides Judy, which is going to pretty hard as it is while I wait for the witching hour of seven. So where were we? I guess we were at the tail end of the questions that our dissection of the concept of hell presented before Judy called."

"Well, let's see," Adam said and then paused. "How about taking the concept a bit further and consider what happens to those who don't believe in hell in any form or fashion, or even a supreme being you keep calling God. What happens to them when they die?"

"I can only speculate," I replied, "since all of my convictions turn on blind faith, and not on any certain knowledge which can be acquired empirically. But I have been wrestling with this moral dilemma for a long time, and I have to believe that these folks will be enlightened in due course within moments of dying, and they will know there is a God and they will understand they can elect to be with Him or reject Him in accordance with their own free will. With full understanding of the incredible being I call God, they more likely than not will embrace his saving grace and elect to be with Him. But they remain free to reject this option and find themselves on the long road to hell. However, I am also convinced that they still will have a chance to redeem themselves later and ask to get out of hell and finally be with our ever merciful Father."

"Yeah, sounds nice," Adam said, "but as you say you are only speculating, so the question remains in my mind is: Could I go to hell if I never believed in its existence, and choose not to believe in it even after I may come face to face with God. I mean, don't we have enough of hell here on earth, assuming there is such a concept that could even be labeled hell? And can I reject both hell as a concept in the supernatural world and not go there, while at the same time reject God as well? Maybe go to a sort of limbo, a comfortable place to be sure, where I would be neither in heaven nor hell."

"Good question, old buddy. We used to preach a status of being in limbo for centuries, but that was mostly to scare the shit out of people who refused to get baptized, especially in the Catholic Church. But the Church has backed off the limbo thing. And I don't know if there really could be such a place, especially for all doubting folks who would want the better of two alternatives. No heaven, but no hell either. Just a land of luxury without having to sing all those praises to the God Almighty all day," I admonished.

"Yeah, well as I read you," Adam countered, "I can't help but wonder what the hell is there to believe in if one doesn't have to conform to the rules here on earth, and yet be able to get into heaven by choosing to accept the gift of salvation right at the end. Couldn't Hitler have done this? Stalin, etc.? If Hitler bears responsibility for the death of six million Jews, and maybe some of the 54 million other people who died as a result of World War II, does this mean he should never be able to get out of hell even if he wants to later on? Or maybe not even go there if he saw the light at the moment of death and repented and accepted the gift of salvation. And how about if he only killed one million Jews, does that gruesome, terrible, lesser number but still egregiously severe misconduct, translate into a term of years in hell in human time rather than to burn forever in God time?

"And how about the others who at first choose hell over God, but sooner or later repent. Can an all-merciful God keep anyone in hell, even a Hitler, once they see the light and repent and beg to be with Him. Is there anything one can do, however bad, that would keep him in hell once he realized the evil of his ways and the foolishness of choosing at an earlier point not to be with God?"

"Also, how likely is it," Adam pressed on, "that someone would continue to reject God, even in the face of the awesome despair and knowledge that he has rejected God and this could keep him in hell forever, even after realizing the terrible mistake his earlier rejection of God was? Seems most unlikely. And in this context, I also ought to address the ultimate example – which may sound a bit ironic – but couldn't Lucifer repent and ask for salvation and a return to heaven after millions or maybe the billions of years that he has been the

Prince of Hades with a mission to corrupt souls so they would reject God and His all merciful salvation?"

I was about to try and answer Adam's difficult scenario when the phone rang again. It was Judy. "Just called to say goodnight again. I can't stop thinking about our date for this evening. You must think I'm nuts, but I wanted to confirm that this is not a hasty decision, and it has been a struggle to resist this long."

"I appreciate your honesty," I answered gently, "and I'm glad you called because I need to clarify something that has been troubling me since we talked a few minutes ago. It's got to do with whether or not I have pressured you unrealistically in my pursuit of seduction. I just need you to feel comfortable in the fact that nothing will change my mind about how I feel for you whether or not we make love as completely as I would like, or if we don't at all. It's not mandatory. I want our first time to be something we both choose. Not just me. I will respect whatever decision you make, and I assure you I will respect you afterwards, whichever way you decide."

"That's sweet of you, Pat, and I appreciate your saying so," Judy answered.

"Oh, and one more thing," I jumped in. "I want you to know that I do love you. I had never said it before tonight, but I realize that I do, and it's the right time to say so. And I will continue to love you no matter how much or how little we do in the lovemaking department tonight. Okay?"

"Thank you, Pat. That means so much to me. And before I hang up, I think you ought to know, I feel the same. So, if to say I love you is no longer premature in our intimate relationship, consider it said. I love you. See you tonight. Sleep well. I'm not making any promises, but you may need a lot of energy. Bye."

I chuckled as I hung up. Adam asked what the hell this second call was all about, but he also noted he wasn't surprised that I had told Judy I loved her and he was certain I did. I simply smiled and said something to the effect that the call was about time.

"About time? What the hell does that mean?" he asked.

"Adam, my friend, it means that it is like finally figuring out that hell doesn't have to be forever, assuming there is such a place. And people can be given the chance to change their minds. No matter how truly evil one has been, hope can still spring eternal, and in time we all can follow our hearts and souls in their first intention that is directed to God. Time allows us to do timely things, like loving completely, and undoing a lot of bad karma we have accrued. A season for everything so to speak, including returning to the Godhead from which we sprang into this life, or many lives before this, or even many to follow. And maybe this answers your question we were weighing when Judy called a minute ago. It's all about love and choices, and time. So open us a couple more beers and we'll talk about things other than hell, which I am satisfied I have personally figured out, and hopefully you have too. Instead let's talk about your love life; a perfect example for reflecting on how time will deliver you too," I added with a big grin. "But we have focused on my perspectives and love life enough, now let's talk about yours."

"Well let me see," Adam started. "There's this really fine looking girl, Cindy, and she too has big, lovely, incredibly, inviting boobs. And, wow, do I want to get to the point where you have so comfortably brought Judy. Maybe you should write me a script," he added with more than a little hope in his voice and a hell of a lot of desire.

"Can't do that, Adam lad. This is something that you must do from the heart, even if clumsy at first. Notice that is spelled heart, not hard, so there is no script that can make it sound sincere except to just say it like you feel. Be genuine.

“Women can see through bullshit. They get exposed to it every day by guys who couldn’t finesse a piece of ass outside of a whorehouse. Be your charming, but sincere self, and Cindy will come around.

“Honest to God!”

The End

I'LL REMEMBER APRIL

I felt like I should be apologizing to Bill Holden and Jennifer Jones for intruding on their special high and windy hill where they discovered strong desire coursing in their hearts and souls in the amorous movie, *Love Is A Many–Splendored Thing*. The hill - with its wild, wind bent tree - overlooked Repulse Bay and not Hong Kong Harbor, as the director of the movie wanted the viewers to believe. But it was nonetheless a most romantic spot accentuated by gorgeous vistas of the Hong Kong area. And I was there, absent Holden and Jones, but very much in love as they were in that wonderfully, passionate film.

It was April 1968, and I had survived the Tet Offensive in Nam. My R&R was only six days, but I was going to make the most of it before I had to go back to the lst Marine Division for another six months of what I was afraid could be the rest of my life. If I made it that long.

April was my first choice for R&R after almost three months on the line mopping up from the blood bath of Tet, and I sought that special month because it was the month on my life's calendar in which three magical occasions blessed me with the greatest joys of my life, none of which occasions were otherwise related. Those special happenings brought a trio of extraordinary women to me in April of various years, the first starting when I was twenty and about to finish my third year of college.

My fourth year would be put on hold since in the summer of 1950 a war suddenly made a terrible entry into my world and I found myself in Korea as a brand new Marine following boot camp. September 1950 saw me climbing over the sea wall at Inchon with a lot of other green kids. Fortunately, we were supported by a number of battle hardened Marines from World War II. But this is not a war story. We won the Korean War, or police action as pinhead Harry Truman called it. So at least the South Korean people remained free and prospered over the many years that followed. In this narrative I simply use my two wars, Korea and Vietnam, as points of reference in what is my love story that started in April 1950, and blossomed in two other Aprils that made that month so very unique.

The first April magic found me impossibly in love with a classmate at the university we attended. The only problem was that the gorgeous object of all my passion and love was engaged to another student. This other guy had graduated the previous semester, and he was away undergoing extended training for a spot with a big corporation in a city across the country far from the university. I used to joke around with the lady, who I knew was sort of promised to the distant guy. And one day I suggested that if she ever was lonely or whatever, I would be happy to fill in so to speak for what she might need.

What I didn't know was that she needed to be certain if maybe she ought to have at least one different experience of the male/female type before she completely tied herself down. Thus I was surprised when she called me two nights before Spring break and suggested that, if I didn't have any other plans, maybe we could slip away to the lake region and spend a few days together. I would have cancelled a private audience with the Pope to spend that promised time with her, and we did as she suggested. Five incredible days of sun, fun, and lovemaking like there was no tomorrow.

Our idyllic retreat had to end, of course, but the lovemaking did not, and upon our return to the university, we managed to meet with increasing regularity to continue our delightfully forbidden affair.

Which I found to be some of the best there is, the forbidden kind that is, and what started that April in which I fell impossibly in love, continued to the end of the semester.

But it all came crashing down when the saddest of all goodbyes was thrust upon me as she told me she and the other guy, to whom she had been engaged, were actually married, having eloped several months earlier, and he was only waiting for her to finish the year so she could move to wherever the hell he was. A minor point she failed to mention when we immersed ourselves in our love odyssey during Spring break. Not that I would have cared, because I wanted her something fierce and I wouldn't care if she had ten husbands at the time. But I hadn't planned to fall in love with the lady, although I did. Head over heals, as the old saying goes.

"I'm sorry," I think I heard her say over and over between her tears and mine, to which she added more than once, "I made a bad decision, but now I believe I have to live with it. I know I will have many regrets, but not one moment of those will be about my having loved you even for this little while and tasted what I know I will never have again. I am so sorry for the pain this inflicts on you and on me. But I have to give the marriage a try.

"I owe it to him. And you and I cannot go forward together. But I'll always look back and remember you as the true light of my life. I will always love you, my darling."

I looked at the lovely face I was so absorbed with and at her delightful body, which I had enjoyed in every way possible, but I couldn't say good-bye. Just, "I'll be seeing you, and I'll try like hell to understand even a little of this. I love you. Nothing can change that and I doubt if I could ever find love again without you." With that I turned away and with all my will I tried to keep from looking back. But I failed, and I turned for one last heart-breaking look at my lost love. That June, when we parted, I joined the Marine Corps to run away more than anything else. Which was an ironic time to be running away since quite unexpectedly the North Koreans took on a great deal of my attention as they crossed the 38th parallel in Korea and invaded the South. War has a tendency to keep one occupied, but I could never forget that wonderful April and my first real love. I thought it could never be better than that.

After a year and a half in Korea and fortunate to stay alive in spite of spending a few weeks in the Naval Hospital at Yokusuka, Japan recovering from some serious wounds that gratefully had left my manhood in tact, I returned to the United States and finished my enlistment at Camp Pendleton, California. Every weekend I dallied with young women, especially in Laguna Beach, who appreciated U. S. Marines in delightful ways. Many of them were sweet and very generous with themselves, but there were no new April beginnings as I finished my enlistment and returned to my final year of college, four years after my first great April experience had ended.

It was towards the end of my last year at the university that I had occasion to travel to a New York system university in upstate New York where I met the second of my April loves. At the same time I discovered that not only could I love again, but even more deeply than I would have believed possible after parting so sadly four years earlier from my first April enchantment. I spotted her in a choral group that was entertaining the out of state members of our national fraternity on our first day of the convention.

I couldn't stop focusing on her face and figure. Such delights. Damn, I thought, if I can't keep my eyes off of her, how in the hell am I going to keep my hands off of her? Provided I can even get next to her. But I managed, and after the concert I went straight for the juggler as I approached her with probably the worst line I could have used. “Hi! I want to apologize for staring at you all through your performance, but I have to admit the only thing better than your singing is your fabulous looks. And quite frankly I just had to meet you. So if you want me to shut up and move along, I will. But only with the greatest reluctance.”

“Well, that’s quite an opening,” she replied with a most disarming smile, “but I’ll overlook the obvious and say thank you, and add that I don’t want you to move on, at least until I know enough about you to determine whether I want you to stay longer or less.”

That’s how it started, but I didn’t fall in love at first sight, although damn near. The lady was fabulous, and more importantly, she thought I was too, although she didn’t say so at first. The next six days were filled with bullshit fraternity meetings and other functions, many of which I deliberately missed, because, when the lady was not in class, we both played hooky and would drive over to a nearby lake and picnic and tell stories, and ask questions about each other. Then before long, we made love, before, during, and after falling in love. Another April, another lake. How they seemed to go together in my love life.

I had to wrench myself away when the week was over to return to the university and finish the last couple months before graduation. I told the lady for whom I now professed undying love, that I would be back in June for a further visit right after graduation. In the meanwhile we kept the letters and phone calls carrying our burning love back and forth, always promising to be loving each other eternally. The day after graduation I returned to her and we spent three glorious weeks inside each other as deeply as two lovers ever could be. Then once again I had to say a tearful goodbye as I left to go back to the Marine Corps a second time, and I reported to Marine Corps Base, Quantico, Virginia where I was slated to go through ten weeks of the Officer Candidate Course.

We saw each other most weekends, however, as I progressed through the officer program and then six months of The Basic School after commissioning. I would either meet the lady in New York City or she would fly down to Washington for the loveliest of reunions in the venerable old Williard Hotel. We loved as if there were no tomorrow, but tomorrow arrived anyway. The end of Basic School, where the Corps tried to make real Marines out of new shave tail lieutenants, and quite frankly succeeded quite well, came on much too quickly.

Having lived through enlisted status during the Korean War, I tried a little harder than most of the others and ended up first, both in Officer Candidate Class and in The Basic School. As a result, I was offered a regular commission in the United States Marine Corps, and I jumped at the chance without consulting my lady. I thought that she would be as proud as I was, especially because she knew how much I loved the Corps.

When I broke the news while on leave before my next assignment, which was to the 3rd Marine Division, Fleet Marine Force, in Japan, my lady was proud of me, but definitely not thrilled that first, I was going away for thirteen months to Japan without her, and secondly, I was planning to make a career out of the Marine Corps. I was surprised, but as I look back on it, I can now understand. And she was right when she sagely observed that the life of a military wife is a highly demanding calling, and not every woman can make it, no matter how well intentioned she might be.

“Don’t decide right now,” I suggested, well actually I begged more than suggested, because I didn’t want to give up my serious desire to spend thirty years in the Corps while at the same time lose my dear love. "I'll write as often as possible, and I'll be home in thirteen months. God how long that sounds, and then we'll get married. You have two more years of college, so I guess you wouldn't want to be married while I'm gone, and regrettably the Marine Corps will not allow me to take you with me on this tour even if we were married."

"I understand," she replied, "and I'll see how it goes. I never expected this when I fell in love with you. You talked about the Marines in a past tense and never suggested you were going back in to make a career. But I won't make any hasty decisions. Let's both think about our future while you are gone."

"Fair enough," I answered with a lot of fear in my heart. "And I'll be even more fair and grudgingly suggest that maybe you should date others at school while I'm away. But I mean date in a very proper sense, my love. And not in an intimate sense. You are mine exclusively as long as you want to be, and the same goes for me. But socialize and see if I am the guy you are willing to make a life with in an environment you never gave a thought to before. Then when I get back we'll set a wedding date if you will still have me, but you will have to accept the fact that the Corps will be a major focus in our lives, and you will be moving around a lot. Plus there will be other separations in peace, and maybe in war, that you wouldn't have if you settled down with some other guy whose life style is more stable. You know, things like marriage, houses with picket fences, and lots of kids. Do what you need to while I am gone, and we'll take it from there. I love you, and always will, even if you marry some other jerk. Sorry, didn't mean that to come out that way. If you marry anyone else, I'm sure he'll be terrific, but to me he'll still be a jerk."

"Well, that was quite a speech Lieutenant, but I appreciate the analysis, and I'll just see how it goes while you are in the Land of the Rising Sun, and I am still struggling to complete my degree in education and become a teacher, which is something I guess I've always wanted as much as you wanted to be a Marine."

With that, we spent our last night together. The last one ever, and we made love in a way that found desperate passion tinged with sadness. In the morning I left with a terrible sense of foreboding and a very heavy heart. While I was overseas, the lady pressed me several times to resign my commission and settle down without any prospect of being uprooted at the pleasure of the President, so we could have a nice safe family life. I declined, and asked if someone else had made her the offer she suggested to me. She replied in a letter - the kind we called a "Dear John" - that she had, but she was torn between her love for me, and her appreciation of everything this other guy was and stood for. I answered that she should do what was in her best interest in the context of life long plans, and she did. Sent me a last letter that said she was getting engaged to the other guy – the jerk as I called him – and wished me every good thing in life including a new love which could be as good as ours was.

I called when I got back and she told me of her wedding plans, so I decided I wouldn't go to New York for one last chance at saving what we had. She understood and I never saw her again. But I also never stopped loving her, any more than I stopped loving my first lady love who decided she had to stay with her husband. Knowing I would always remember my loves of April, I was not certain that the next time, if there were any, I would ever be able to love like them again.

My next duty station was at Headquarters Marine Corps in Washington, D.C., which actually is in Arlington, Virginia. I would have preferred an assignment once again to Camp Pendleton and an infantry regiment, but someone who either liked me or didn't care what I wanted, decided a tour at Headquarters would be a good ticket punch for an up and coming Marine lieutenant with a substantial war record. So I reported into Headquarters and was assigned to combat plans and operations development. It was a very interesting job and the nice thing about duty at the head shed was that, when I didn't have to stand the watch as assistant staff duty officer, all weekends were free, and that meant more time than I probably needed to socialize with the ton of lovely women who made up a large portion of the folks who graced the D.C. scene. But nothing spectacular was happening in the love department, and I wasn't giving it a whole lot of help since the ache for the would be teacher who was marrying the jerk still loomed large, as well as the warm memories of the special love from my college days. The boy meet girl scenarios consisted of a real cornucopia of pretty faces, and some generous bodies, so I went with the flow without serious involvement.

A year later one of my Marine friends with whom I had served in Japan invited me to an Easter Sunday dinner with his family, and he asked if it would all right to invite a young teacher who was currently teaching his daughter in first grade. I said fine, but no matchmaking.

He rogered that and I showed up for dinner in another special April, at which moment my life and love pursuits took a new and exciting turn. The teacher was a lovely woman, with long dark brown hair and big brown eyes. Her eyes were very much like the would be teacher in New York who dear John'd me while I was in Japan because I wouldn't bail out of the Corps and settle down to her version of hearth and home. They brought back wonderful and yet some painful memories as well.

I was immediately attracted to my non-matchmaking date, but not sure whether it was the long beautiful legs, her great breasts, or her smile that melted me with my first glance at this remarkable woman with the wonderful eyes, and all the rest of her. Whatever it was, I knew intuitively that this was destined to be one of those spontaneous, special April experiences, and sooner or later the lovely teacher and I were going to become an item.

Which in Marine Corps jargon meant I definitely will be seducing this great looking woman, but this time it wasn't going to be one of those bonk her and then say thank you ma'am deals. This one I vowed to handle with patience and finesse, and I promised to start thinking with the head on my shoulders, and not the one between my legs. It was to be slow and easy. No frantic effort to replace the loves I found in the other two Aprils and then lost. I was not even going to think about falling in love early on with this new discovery. Slow and easy, and if in the end it didn't work, I was convinced I could just walk away without a broken heart.

The Easter dinner went well, and I began to appreciate that the teacher was more than just a very fine looking package. She was very bright, articulate, outgoing, and quite pleasant all around. My friend had picked her up at her place and brought her to his home for the dinner realizing that I would be in a position to drive her home later if we hit it off, and it would give us a chance to spend some time alone to get to know each other better.

The tactic worked well, and the teacher and I talked comfortably on the drive to her place and then a whole lot more after she invited me in for a nightcap. The only difference was that in the company of the other folks at dinner, she was a bit more guarded than when we were alone. We were talking just one on one when she gave me a certain look and she seemed to focus on my facial and other body language in order to assess whether I was being candid in some comment or two or if I was giving her a line of crap. I liked the look immediately because it told me this exciting woman was not going to be a pushover and that she clearly was not going to tolerate any bullshit from anyone, including me, if I wanted us to become an item.

"I'd like to get to know you better, and hope we can start with a date this coming weekend. I realize that teaching is a demanding profession and you are busy during the week, but maybe you can work me in for Friday or Saturday night," I asked perhaps a bit too cautiously.

"Sounds good," she replied. "I had a tentative date for Saturday, but I told him I would have to see and would let him know by Wednesday. Now I will let him know that it is no date. I won't tell him it's because I would rather be with a Marine, which he would hate since he is a Navy type. But he'll live."

"Hey, good idea. No point in giving him more reason to be jealous of Marines. How about dinner and some dancing? Pick you up about seven?"

"Sounds fine. It's a date."

"Now, if I may," I added, "I'd like to intrude a tad on your privacy, but if you don't want to answer, no sweat."

"All right, go ahead."

"For openers, since you are so damned lovely, I was wondering why you aren't already taken, like married or something. I see no wedding ring or engagement ring."

"I can answer that without my privacy being violated," teacher answered. "I was married. Straight out of college. I am 24 years old, and that was when I was 21. It lasted three years, more or less. More less than more. It was all wrong, but it took a while to accept that. I worked at it, and maybe he did too, but it didn't take, and so I have filed for divorce, and next month it should be a done deal. And now I'm free to date, and do what I want with anyone I choose except get married right at the moment, but I doubt if marriage was what you had in mind with the question."

"Touché," I came back. "Sorry things didn't work our for you, but glad for my sake. This way I got to meet you, and hopefully get to know you better without worrying about some irate husband stalking me."

"Oh, he wouldn't do that. I think in some ways it has sunk in with him that this is better for both of us, and we have parted fairly amicably. No kids to worry about either, so that's a blessing as well.

And now that you have found out about me, how about you? No wife? Kids? Fiancée? Or whatever?"

"Right on all of the above. There is none of any, and as to the whatever part, I am a blatant heterosexual, so I've known a woman or two in my life, but no attachments at this time. I had some disappointments, of course, and I haven't been looking for a relationship of serious depth for quite a while. But perhaps it's time. I don't know, and I don't want to come on like gangbusters even though you are as pretty as they come and apparently bright as hell to boot. My kind of woman. So I'd like to see more of you. No pun intended. And see what comes of it. For some strange reason that I can't divine, I felt something that might be solid between us the minute we met. Not love at first sight and all that baloney, but a rapport that seemed to be there even before we had spoken but a few words to each other. Hell, I don't know. I only felt this way twice in my life, and things went well each time until intervening causes shot down what had been so good. I don't know how to phrase it any better than this. Time is on our side.

"You live here and the Marine Corps, absent a sudden war, has advised me that I was likely to stay here in Washington for another three years, so it gives us a lot of time to get to know each other even better if we want to."

"Boy! You are direct, I see. But to tell you the truth I had the same strange feeling when I saw you, and it's not just your looks, which I think are extraordinary. It's something a whole lot more than chemistry in this instance. So I'll go along with your projections, one date at a time. And see where it takes us."

With that I said, "I'd better go," and I extended my hand. Teacher looked at me with her lovely smile, and said, "I think I'll be safe with a kiss goodnight on our first date, if you'd like to give me one. I promise I'll be on my best behavior, and I just know you will too," she teased.

I kissed her, not passionately at first, but serious enough so that it only took a nanosecond to realize I wanted more, and she knew it too. So she pulled her head back and smiled and said, "More where that came from, but not tonight. Thanks for a wonderful first meeting and I look forward to Saturday with enthusiasm."

"Me too," I said like a schoolboy getting his first kiss. "Me too. Goodnight, and thanks."

And so it began, and it got better and better. After a few dates, during which we both realized we wanted more intimacy than just kisses and lots of hugs, we segued into our first full lovemaking along a cozy lake in Virginia. We were alone, shielded by a woods near the water. We chose this particular, isolated setting, because the teacher said she loved to make love outdoors as she lay naked on the cool grass breathing in the sweetness the earth. So we did. It was everything she suggested and sweeter than I had imagined in any fantasy.

That wonderful beginning extended over the next three years during which we saw each other exclusively. We took in every fine restaurant in the D.C. area, and visited most tourist attractions, and delighted in the National Gallery of Art, and the many other galleries, along with every inch of the Smithsonian. We also made trips to New York City for plays and great food, and also took trips to Hawaii, San Francisco, and Hong Kong, and wherever else we could when the Marine Corps let me take my full complement of 30 days leave a year, a couple weeks at a time, to accommodate the teacher's schedules.

We lived in our own apartments, but spent so much time staying in one or the other that we felt like we were actually living together. My lady was a seriously religious Episcopalian and we alternated between the National Cathedral in Washington, and a Roman Catholic Church in Virginia with regularity on Sundays. Our love for each other was not influenced or disturbed by any consideration of immorality. How could it? And we also never gave a thought to the time when the Corps would tap me for a new duty station, more likely than not, once again overseas in Okinawa or Japan.

Then the word came that I definitely was going overseas, but not to the Orient. Instead I had been designated for an all expense paid vacation to exotic Southeast Asia, aka Vietnam, where things had gotten hot and heavy starting in the Spring of 1965. Ah yes! Another April, but not the kind I preferred. A few Marines had been in country as advisors since 1961, but in ’65 we moved into Vietnam in force with the First Marine Division.

That Division landed at Red Beach eight miles North of Da Nang. I was hoping for a return to the lst Division, but when the orders came for me to head to the enchanted land of the South Vietnamese, it was to the Third Marine Division along the DMZ in the I Corps. And I went. For thirteen months.

I was involved in quite a bit of combat, and the reprise of my memories of Korea, which I had left some 13 years earlier, came back in a rush. But I survived, and got back alive and in one piece. I called my lady the minute I got off the plane in California and we met in Washington the next day. The homecoming was fabulous and I thought I could never find so much relief and joy as we experienced in that reunion.

I wish it could have culminated with an announcement that I was returning to Washington for duty, but the Corps saw fit to assign me to the Second Marine Division in Camp Lejeuene, North Carolina, not a continent away, but far enough that not seeing each other more than twice a month was the consequence. But we managed, and it was wonderful, especially in the summer when she was able to stay with me in Jacksonville, and we were together every night for two and half months.

I loved her with an intensity I didn't think possible. I asked her to marry me, and she agreed. The wedding was planned for December at the Fort Myer chapel, and she would join me after finishing the current semester on her teaching contract. I felt like I was in heaven.

The hardest thing was always in our parting, but this time after our glorious summer, the time wasn't that long until we married. And my lady had to get back to teaching for the rest of the semester and planning our wedding. She would be busy, and I'd miss her, but it was for good reason. We would be married before too long, and then no more separations. Just before she left to drive back, I held her tightly and kissed her with deep meaning after looking into her fabulous eyes filled with love. "I am truly happy my darling. December cannot come soon enough. I had looked so long for you, and finally my search has ended. I love you so very much."

My teacher lady waved one last goodbye as she headed out on her way back to Washington still enraptured from the splendor of our summer paradise.

She never got there. Her car was hit head-on by a drunk driver and she was killed instantly. I was grateful she didn't suffer, but the loss was more than I could bear. I took leave and made arrangements with her family for her funeral. We buried her in the family plot, and I was overwhelmed with a sadness I believed would never depart.

I went back to Camp Lejeune and volunteered for another tour in Vietnam. It was a death wish, of course, and I was speedily allowed to do so because the war had escalated substantially, and combat experienced officers were a must. So I was in the right place at the right time. I was assigned to my old division, the lst Marine Division, FMF, and arrived in Nam in late December 1967. A month later Tet '68 kicked off and we fought many bloody battles until it was fully determined that the North Vietnamese and the Viet Cong had bitten off more than they realized.

When things finally got back to some semblance of normal, whatever that might have been considered in Nam in 1968, I was allowed R&R to Hong Kong. Which I chose because my lady and I had been there a few years earlier. We loved each other passionately while we were there, and we would lie on our special hill far from the rest of the world.

So I went back to the hill – our hill under our tree – and I looked at the sky as we had in those golden days of our love when we had filled ourselves with the joy that only lovers totally alone in their private world can know completely uninhibited by other concerns.

It was this special place, filled with memories of her and our love, which found me on our hill during my R&R from Nam, with tears streaming down my face as I remembered her and the love that started in April much too little time ago.

I also gave thought to the other loves I had found in April twice before, and sadly reflected how cruel life can be to have loved so much and then lost so terribly.

I dried my eyes as best I could, and then I took a notebook from my pocket and composed a poem dedicated to the collective memory of the three magnificent women who I first loved in April. And always would. It reads:

April and You

Not one solitary day has passed

Since that last lovely night

When we made love for a final time,

That I have not found

My heart pressed to your breast.

That summer night when we clung
Desperately to the denial of
Tomorrow, so that the pain of nevermore,
Could not chill the joy of loving
Without reservation.

Not one day moves on that
I do not think of you, warmed by the memory
of our love.

While in the same instant,
I ache with indescribable torment
Over the loss of the tangible
Realization of that love, and all of its sensory and
Spiritual magnificence.

We first loved in April In an earlier time and place
In what seems like a lifetime ago.
It was a lovely spring day along a lake.
Ah where did it go?

I will always remember April –

and cherish the warm, loving memory of each of you,

And my heart will smile.

The End

DOIN' IT FOR SOME DOLL

Had a friend. Dumb bastard. Got married three times. Was engaged a few more in addition. Maybe he was lucky to escape with only three wives, since he couldn't think with the head on his shoulders when the one on the other end was jerking him along in all the wrong directions, at all the wrong times.

So what was the "other root "of his problem? Well, the question drives the answer. But simply put, no decision of any consequence which rose above the level of I'm hungry, what should I eat, ever entered into his thinking unless some doll, or gal, lass, fair maiden, broad, babe, chick, fluff, vamp, or whatever else you want to call a girl or woman, political correctness notwithstanding, was the dominant determining factor in the equation.

He loved women, or girls as he referred to them from time to time depending on his age. From five years on he loved all the "girls" he could get his hands on. Until he turned sixteen. Then he loved all the "women" he could get his hands on. Literally. And there was nothing he wouldn't do for them if they asked, as long as the quid pro quo had a direct relationship to his lusty passions. This guy was the prototype for the old cliché that warns: "He would screw a snake if someone held its head."

Nothing new about this and the dope's dilemma circumscribing his inability to reason with a hard on. World's full of dumb shits like him. Maybe most men at one time or another. Or maybe, all the time.

So what I need to address in light of my normal or abnormal friend, whichever you prefer, is what happened to Mick, other than that which would be expected due to his inherent male weakness, like getting his assed kicked and his heart broken from time to time.

My friend started his odyssey with female types in grade school. It was mostly just kissing and fooling around. Until first year high school, that is, when he found out that his desire to cop a feel had certain risks associated. But he ultimately also discovered that sweet talk, sweetened with material offerings, produced better results, and reduced the risk factor substantially. Just little things at first, like charm bracelets from county or state fairs. But small trinkets segued into larger bobbles and bangles, like expensive jewelry, or items of clothing, which usually wiped out his savings. It allowed him, however, to use his middle digit as a reconnaissance finger, and he soon learned to explore the female in ways far more enjoyable than merely copping a feel. These were decidedly more interesting.

Such pursuits left him substantially aroused but incomplete so to speak, with enough sperm backed up to give him a whiteout. Thus by the time he turned sixteen, he was making trips to a rural area, fully protected by the local county sheriff where women of more advanced procedures introduced him to the delightful deed. And he graduated to a loss of his remaining innocence with enthusiastic devotion.

It was during one of his visits to a house of commercial affection that his first real problem with love for sale came down on him big time. He had a favorite comfort lady named, Toby, not much older than he, who he usually sought out in that particular pleasure palace whenever possible. Which means whenever he had the going rate for pussy delight.

This always gave him two shots for the price of one. Hell, he was young and, although his staying power was under developed at the tender age of 16, his recovery time was exceptional. Unfortunately, the other clienteles' interest in the young and tender, Toby, allegedly 18, was not limited to my horny friend. She had, among others, a regular overnighter who was usually drunk on his ass when he arrived, and, if not, he was soon afforded that opportunity at the bar downstairs separate from the "do the dirty deed department" upstairs. Thus the madam was able to extract large sums of the drunken jerk's stash for his all nighters with Toby. Which actually consisted of less action in six hours than my erotic buddy, Mick, got in an hour.

One night while my numb nuts friend was still within his hour of enjoying all sorts of delicious carnal conversation with Toby, the drunk shows up and demands action. When the madam said it would only be a few minutes, the asshole charges up to Toby's domain and catches Mick having seconds with the lady of their mutual interest. The drunk then made the second major mistake of the night and decided to pull Mick off of Toby, for which my bud, who stood six feet and weighed a solid, no body fat, 195 pounds, with a golden gloves light heavy championship at sixteen, beat the crap out of the drunk and threw him down the stairs.

The proprietor of the whorehouse took a dim view of this and ordered my amigo to get dressed, leave, and never come back. And also to pay $200 damages to a coffee table the drunk smashed when he landed on it, plus the easy $100 she could have separated from the drunk as he slept off his condition in Toby's bed, while in a spare bedroom she worked some other clients who sought her tender loins. Mick had to sell his old jalopy to pay the bill, but with an extra $100.00 kicker, he was allowed guest privileges once more, while the drunk was banned for life. I asked Mick why he would do that, and he simply said he was doing it for the doll. Quite an experience at 16, but then he said he was used to doing nice things for ladies, even at a cost of his worldly goods, because that's what a gentleman does. What a dunce.

And so it went with my mick friend, and he visited Toby with regularity, but as time passed he did so less and less because he became enamored with a sweet young thing from a private girls' high school, and they developed into an item. Which is a euphemism for what was a lot of hugging and grabbing, which ineluctably became more penetrating. And this was accepted as all right since they allegedly loved each other, and the old joke about nice Catholic girls using an aspirin for birth control by holding one tightly between the girl's closed knees, gave way to doing what came naturally.

It took two years of this kind of foolishness for Mick to knock up his honey bun. Her folks, being Catholic and absolutely opposed to abortion, legal or illegal, saw to it that Mick and his lady fair with the growing tummy got married. Mick said it was O.K. because that's what a gentleman does for a doll when he fires live shots at her plumbing. What a dunce.

As you can imagine, the marriage lasted in reality only a couple of months, but a little longer in fact, until the lady suffered a miscarriage, so Mick was off the hook and soon they were divorced. Mick, in the meanwhile, dropped in on his old brothel beat, but Toby wasn't there. She had been knifed to death in a fight with a John who accosted her in the city when he professed an inability to live without her, and he didn't want her to be with any other men ever again. The asshole did her in, and then himself. Sad loss for the world with Toby's departure. No loss, however, with the overdue demise of the obsessed lunatic, the John who couldn't live "without her, or with anything else," including himself.

Mick searched for a replacement for Toby, but he decided whoring around wasn't the best way to go, so he looked for and found a steady, who after a bit of coaxing and a ton of Mick's charm, serviced him with delight and frequency, and vice versa. That is when she could get away from home, because her husband was really narrow minded about such conduct, and the lady didn't want to lose her inheritance or her interim security of fancy home and cushy bank accounts.

Of course, Mick couldn't compete in the way of material comforts but he did relish his sexual provider role. He said it made him feel really good to be able to do it for the doll. Only problem was that one afternoon he was doing it to, and as he claims, for the doll, foolishly this time, in her marital bed when her hubby was supposed to be out of town. Just as Mick was finishing the doll for a third time, he heard four of the most terrifying words a man can hear when in the wrong bed at the wrong time: "Hi honey, I'm home."

The guy was very upset over his discovery of the assignation of his wife with a kid, a handsome Irish looking guy, so he immediately went to the top drawer of his dresser, got a gun and shot Mick somewhere between Mick reaching for his clothes and trying to figure if the window or the door was the best exit. Mick lived, and the D.A. nol-prossed the assault with a deadly weapon charge. Figuring Mick had it coming.

Which is a punny play on words since Mick had it coming - as in really coming - for a couple of years with the guy's wife. Mick said no more of that married stuff. Too dangerous, and then he got hooked up with another nice girl; single, quite pretty, with big boobs. One night while he was lying through his teeth and ejaculating from other body parts, he proclaimed he loved his lady of the moment, and she suggested in that event they should get married. Exhausted and certain he didn't want to do that, but afraid to lose this highly sensuous siren, he agreed.

Two weeks later, no time for formalities for that doll, they eloped to Vegas and were married by a smashingly, beautiful woman preacher named, Reverend Marlys, in the Rio Hotel and Casino wedding chapel. The arrangement lasted eight months, and then they separated. But Mick agreed to pay $600.00 a month as tribute to the lady for the screwing he was about to get, for the screwing he got. He said, "No sweat. I've got a good job, and she was good to me, so I'm doin’ it for the doll." What a dunce.

You'd think this would have cured Mick of any confusion about the so-called bliss of the married state, but it didn't. There were a number of other dolls in between for whom he was doin’ it," but can you believe it - he married again. Nice looking girl from California. Great screw, but clearly from another place in the universe. Sort of like California's Governor Moonbeam, who regularly lived in La La Land.

The marriage lasted six months and then Mick bailed when he finally had to admit his sexy wife was as light in the head as she was heavy in the sex department. The mix was too much even for Mick who loved to bop the lady, but they had a terrible communication thing, which is normal when the parties are from different planets. He gave her the $600 a month he had been giving to his big boobed, ex-wife who had remarried and the spousal support facade had stopped. He said, "What the fuck, I'm doin' it for the doll. Who cares, it's only money. Easy come, easy go." I'm not sure the pun wasn't intentional, but that's what he seemed to believe. What a dunce.

By this time Mick was 25 years old, and still looking for someone to hold the snake's head while he screwed it. I knew Mick all of his life. We were neighbors from the day we were born only one month apart, so we grew up doing all kinds of fun things and learning more and more about each other every day. The only thing I didn't fully understand was why he was so horny, and how it kept messing up his life. Of course, he usually had a wide smile on his face because he was getting so much nooky. Why this was his major avocation in life, however, I hadn't been able to specifically divine.

Before any amateur armchair sex psychologist suggests that Mick suffered from a male nympho syndrome, which the shrinks call "satyriasis or Don Juanism," let me disabuse you of that mistaken idea. Mick was not sexually dysfunctional, in spite of what appears to have been a rather substantial appetite for sexual activity. He actually was no different than most males of any specie. It's just that it was predominant with him, and he didn't make an effort to adjust well to the idea that life without sex could be tolerable. Well okay, maybe just barely tolerable, but his whole focus was on relationships that started and mostly ended with sex. Like the cowboy who got thrown off the bronk, Mick always climbed back on and rode.

Notwithstanding that by the time Mick could have avoided military service since he was almost past draft age, he volunteered and joined the Marine Corps. Which meant he either had a death wish, or he was looking for adventure that might parallel the excitement and challenge of his sexual pursuits. The Corps was willing to accommodate him, and after 12 weeks of boot camp at Parris Island, and some advanced infantry training at Camp LeJeuene,

Mick went to Vietnam, and he fought the good fight with other jarheads for six months. Then he got to go on R&R to Australia.

He deliberately asked for Australia because he heard the Australian women were especially good looking, and really appreciated U.S. Marines because their folks had talked about how swell they had been during World War II. So off he went on a Pan American, R&R flight to Sidney, and he discovered that all the rumors were true and then some. Great looking Aussie girls loved U.S. Marines, and Mick loved them back. He only had six days, but he was going to make the best of it, by making as many of these sportive ladies as possible. He didn't get much sleep, but his enthusiasm for the Aussie lasses' flesh and a few nap sandwiches (that's a little sleep in between two pieces of ass) kept him up and coming.

Upon his return to Vietnam, Mick's Company Commander said, "Welcome home. From the looks of you, I suspect you will have to get back in the war to get a little rest," the good-natured young Captain joshed. "Whad'ya do, fuck every Aussie Sheila who signaled that her golden valley would be open to you because you are a big, brave, handsome Marine?"

"Yes, Sir," Mick replied with a grin. "You must have been to Australia yourself."

"I haven't been," the Captain answered, "but with your obvious body language recommendation, you can bet your ass I will. If I live long enough. And speaking of living long, I am sending your platoon out to a village I can't even pronounce the name of, to keep some of our South Vietnamese friends alive."

The Captain then called Mick's platoon leader and advised, "The VC have been giving the CAP a bad time." (CAPS were Combined Action Platoons, which consisted of small contingents of U.S. Marines and a few ARVN soldiers, designed to protect, as well as, help win the hearts and minds of the South Vietnamese people). "And I want your platoon to reinforce the CAP and get down and dirty with every Viet Cong you can find and dispatch each one of the bastards from the planet."

With that order firmly in mind, Mick's platoon leader gathered up his men, some 39 in number, and set out for the village the Captain designated. They met no resistance along the way, but the day after they had reinforced the CAP in the village, the VC launched a mortar and sapper attack in broad daylight. Which was unusual, but it obviously was a ploy to convince the village farmers that the Liberation Front (The Viet Cong) were the true Vietnamese and were determined to lead the followers of Ho Chi Minh to victory over the American imperialists. The attack failed in this regard, and in the end 26 Viet Cong were killed and 15 were captured.

During the attack, however, in the midst of an extended mortar barrage, a terrified young child of three broke out of her mother's arms that had been shielding her in a makeshift bunker inside the village. The child ran in the direction of the line of the incoming mortar rounds. While the VC were falling short in their fire, Mick saw immediately that the child was about to be placed in extreme danger by advancing towards the impact line. So he jumped up and left his safe position and ran to intercept the child.

As he reached the tiny girl, a round hit within thirty feet of Mick and the sweet little child. Mick without hesitation threw himself on the girl, and he caught the full force of the explosion. The girl was miraculously uninjured, but Mick lived only a few minutes after absorbing the devastating impact of fragmented metal singing a song of heroic death.

When the Corpsman got to him, Mick moaned agonizingly, "Damn this hurts like hell." But then, with his last breath, he softly asked, "Is the kid all right?"

When I later heard about all of this, I finally realized that whatever else might have motivated Mick in his relations with the many women he loved with so much passion, and whom he genuinely wanted to please sexually and otherwise, he clearly wasn't always acting solely in the interests of the dolls.

Except for one hot summer day in Nam in 1968. That totally unselfish day when he finally was doin' it "exclusively" for some doll.

I think it made up for all the other dolls. So many in number. I'm sure they would think so too.

The End

About The Author

In a long and distinguished career, Michael Patrick Murray has been a trial attorney, both as a prosecutor and defense counsel, as well as a trial judge and appellate judge, along with serving as a United States Marine during the Korean and Vietnam Wars.

In addition, he has enjoyed extensive teaching experience as a law professor at four different law schools, putting his five university degrees and broad legal experience to good use in the academic venues.

When asked as to what aspect of his experience he enjoys most, Judge Murray advises, "Added to the genuine pleasure of writing about human nature and the law, as well as the challenge this presents, I truly believe it is a close call between studying law, teaching law, and fighting the good fight in court for truly worthy causes, the most important of which are truth and justice—neither of which are mutually exclusive—nor can they stand alone from each other in the courtroom. This is a hard fact that is lost on many lawyers today."

In addition to this anthology of short stories, Judge Murray's well received novels in which the novels' protagonist, Los Angeles criminal law defense counsel, Sean Fitzpatrick O'Ryan, is introduced and continues his dedicate defense of those wrongfully accused of crimes, are entitled *O'Ryan's Law, Murder By Class,* and *Law Is A Jealous Mistress,* published by 1st Books Library.

www.ingramcontent.com/pod-product-compliance
Lightning Source LLC
Chambersburg PA
CBHW031826170526
45157CB00001B/201

* 9 7 8 1 4 0 3 3 7 1 2 9 4 *